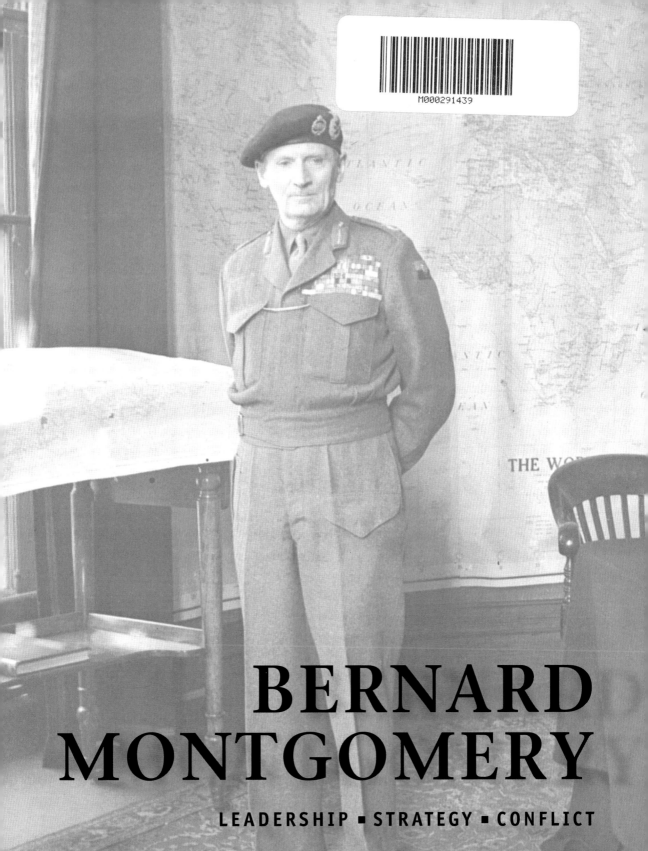

BERNARD MONTGOMERY

LEADERSHIP ▪ STRATEGY ▪ CONFLICT

TIM MOREMAN ▪ ILLUSTRATED BY GRAHAM TURNER

First published in 2010 by Osprey Publishing
Midland House, West Way, Botley, Oxford OX2 0PH, UK
44-02 23rd St, Suite 219, Long Island City, NY 11101, USA

E-mail: info@ospreypublishing.com

ISBN: 978 1 84908 143 6
E-book ISBN: 978 1 84908 144 3

Editorial by Ilios Publishing Ltd, Oxford, UK
www.iliospublishing.co.uk
Cartography by Mapping Specialists Ltd
Page layout by Myriam Bell Design, France
Index by Sandra Shotter
Originated by Blenheim Colour, Eynsham, UK
Printed in China through Worldprint Ltd

10 11 12 13 14   10 9 8 7 6 5 4 3 2 1

A CIP catalogue record for this book is available from the British Library.

Acknowlegment

Many thanks to Mr Robin Boon, Curator of the The King's Royal Hussars
Museum at Winchester, and Mr Mike Galer, Senior Keeper of Military
and Social History at The Regimental Museum of the 9th/12th Lancers,
for providing details about regimental headgear.

Imperial War Museum Collections

The photographs in this book come from the Imperial War Museum's
huge collections, which cover all aspects of conflict involving Britain
and the Commonwealth since the start of the 20th century. These
rich resources are available online to search, browse and buy at
www.iwmcollections.org.uk. In addition to collections online, you
can visit the visitor rooms where you can explore over 8 million
photographs, thousands of hours of moving images, the largest sound
archive of its kind in the world, thousands of diaries and letters written
by people in wartime and a huge reference library. To make an
appointment, call (020) 7416 5320, or e-mail mail@iwm.org.uk.

www.iwm.org.uk

Artist's note

Readers may care to note that the original paintings from which the
colour plates in this book were prepared are available for private sale.
All reproduction copyright whatsoever is retained by the Publishers.
All enquiries should be addressed to:

Graham Turner, PO Box 88, Chesham, Buckinghamshire, UK

The Publishers regret that they can enter into no correspondence upon
this matter.

The Woodland Trust

Osprey Publishing are supporting the Woodland Trust, the UK's leading
woodland conservation charity, by funding the dedication of trees.

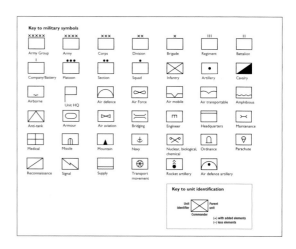

CONTENTS

INTRODUCTION

Field Marshal Bernard Law Montgomery of Alamein (1887–1978) is probably the best known and arguably the most controversial British general of World War II. This idiosyncratic senior officer – known simply as 'Monty' to his adoring men and the star-struck British public – shot to fame from virtual obscurity as GOC (General Officer Commanding) Eighth Army following his decisive victory over Axis forces at El Alamein in October–November 1942. News of this success was trumpeted to the world as showing that the tide of the war had turned against the Axis powers. Following Axis defeat in North Africa, Montgomery helped plan and lead the invasions of Sicily and Italy before returning to the UK at the beginning of 1944. As GOC 21st Army Group and temporary commander of all land forces, Montgomery played a key role in converting a blueprint for Operation *Overlord* into a practicable invasion plan. The ensuing battle of Normandy, moreover, saw Montgomery win a crushing victory that shattered the German Army in the west. Despite a groundswell of criticism from Allied and many British detractors, Monty led 21st Army Group to eventual victory and took the unconditional surrender of German forces in northern Germany at Lüneburg Heath in May 1945.

A portrait of General Bernard Montgomery wearing his trademark black beret with two cap badges taken on 29 May 1943. Montgomery deliberately wore distinctive items of uniform to stand out from other senior officers in the eyes of his troops.

The meteoric rise to fame from virtual obscurity that Montgomery enjoyed from August 1942 surprised a great many of his peers within the British military establishment, who knew him as a rather odd, outspoken and 'unclubbable' outsider who to date had not particularly distinguished himself. Indeed, to those unacquainted with him on first appearance Monty didn't look the part of a soldier, lacking the handsome, inspiring and intimidating physical presence and martial bearing of his peers like Alexander, Auchinleck and Slim. The slightly built and 5ft 7in. Monty was largely the opposite, having a pale, pinched and shrew-like face with a long, sharp, beaky nose, thinning hair and penetrating clear grey-blue eyes. A squeaky,

Montgomery's operations in World War II

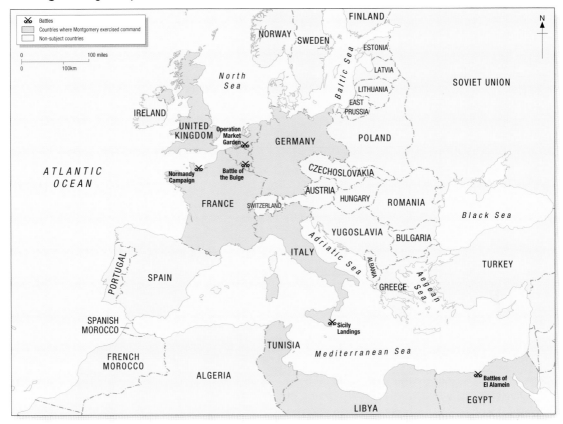

high-pitched and lisping voice further detracted from his image, as arguably did the odd choice of distinctive black beret with two cap badges and a scruffy, workmanlike 'uniform' he carefully later adopted to make himself stand out from his fellow officers. As one of Omar Bradley's aides once wryly remarked, 'With his corduroy trousers, his enormous loose-fitting gabardine coat and his beret' he resembled 'a poorly tailored bohemian painter'.

The reality was much different from this first impression. Montgomery was a charismatic leader and an outstanding field commander, whose experience and years of studying, writing and preparing for a future war marked him out from his amateur peers as a consummate professional. A man of action, Monty always spoke his mind, possessed an innate air of authority and had an obvious determination to win, which quickly disabused those who thought he was not up to the mark. Montgomery was always a soldiers' general who recognized the central importance of morale and developed effective means of establishing an enduring bond of mutual trust and confidence with his officers and men. Overall, Montgomery was an inspirational leader, a skilled trainer of troops and a masterful tactician, whose appreciation of how to conduct warfare under modern conditions made him the most effective general that Britian employed in Northwest Europe during World War II. As Francis de Guingand, his chief of staff from 1942–45, later wrote: 'To anyone

who had been involved with the British Army between 1919 and 1945 he was, undisputedly, the greatest military field commander our nation managed to produce.'

Montgomery had a difficult, awkward and complex personality, however, which proved to be a source of both strength and serious weakness at a high level of command. Indeed, on several occasions it nearly wrecked his career. Monty always exuded single–mindedness, determination and a brimming self-confidence and faith in himself, with an organizational ability, knowledge of modern warfare and ability to enthuse morale that marked him out from his

A Canadian Sherman tank advances through the ruins of Regalbuto in August 1943 during the Sicilian campaign. Montgomery frequently clashed with his US counterpart George S. Patton during the fighting in Sicily and this conflict continued in Northwest Europe.

peers. Indeed, he always believed he could accomplish anything given proper freedom and time to plan. On the other hand Monty was an arrogant, vain and intolerant man who could never admit he was wrong and seldom backed down in an argument when he believed he was right. He lacked social skills. Indeed, the lonely, bitter and socially inept Monty had a gift for arousing jealousy and enmity. A strong vein of cruelty and ruthlessness, moreover, ran through him and was vented upon any officer who stood up against him or failed to live up to Monty's exacting standards. A combination of his egomania, boastfulness and a supercilious manner incensed his critics, especially those from the US eager to make their own mark. These serious character flaws made Monty an extremely difficult colleague and subordinate and made him many enemies during his career. As Lieutenant-General Bedell Smith, Eisenhower's chief of staff, once told Montgomery: 'You may be great to serve under, difficult to serve alongside, but you sure are hell to serve over!'

THE EARLY YEARS

Bernard Law Montgomery was born on 17 November 1887, the third son of the Reverend Henry Montgomery and his young wife Maud (née Farrar), at St Mark's Vicarage, Kennington Oval in South London, where his father was the local clergyman. Bernard was the fourth child of nine eventually born to this staunchly protestant Anglo-Irish family. Both sides of the family had distinguished antecedents. Maud was the daughter of the distinguished Victorian cleric, author and educator Frederic William Farrar, while his paternal grandfather was the distinguished Indian administrator Sir Robert Montgomery, who had made his reputation following the annexation of the

Punjab and the Indian Mutiny. It was not, however, a hugely happy marriage, with the 18-years-younger Maud always the dominant partner. Following his grandfather's death a month after Bernard was born, his father inherited the large ancestral estate of New Park at Moville in County Donegal, located 32km from Londonderry in Ireland. It proved to be a mixed blessing for the family, as a large mortgage that encumbered the estate meant that it proved a permanent heavy financial burden.

The appointment of the Reverend Montgomery as the Anglican Bishop of Tasmania in 1889, when Montgomery was still an infant, provided a financial lifeline for the growing family and for the next 12 years they lived in this small, beautiful and isolated colony. The demands of his new post meant that the kind, frequently bullied and domestically largely ineffectual Bishop Montgomery, whom his son adored, was absent on missionary work for up to six months at a time, leaving his cold, domineering young wife in sole charge of the family and its finances. It was a spartan life for the family living at Bishopscourt (the bishop's official residence in the small town of Hobart, overlooking the picturesque Derwent estuary), with money always in short supply. Left to her own devices, the proud and strong-minded Maud became a strict and fearsome figure with a never-ending series of iron rules imposed upon her progeny, who followed a strict regime each day. The children normally rose at dawn followed by a bedroom inspection and prayers before breakfast commenced, following which tutors from England educated the children in a small schoolroom in the garden. A cold, loveless regime of fierce beatings with a cane administered by their strict mother, being ignored for long periods of time and education by a string of tutors played a major part in Montgomery's upbringing, which he later admitted was 'unhappy'. The rebellious and wilful Montgomery bore the brunt of this harsh regime of corporal punishment meted out by his mother, with whom he deliberately clashed on a regular basis. Monty emerged from this tough ordeal a lonely and rebellious child who was the acknowledged 'black sheep' of the family. This harsh upbringing, moreover, made him fiercely independent and ambitious, but also always at odds with authority.

The Montgomery family briefly returned home to London in 1897 to attend the Lambeth Conference and for a term Bernard and his brother were educated at the King's School at Canterbury. In 1901 Bishop Montgomery reluctantly left Tasmania and permanently returned to London as a reward for his 'evangelical and missionary zeal', when he was appointed secretary of the Society for the Propagation of the Gospel in Foreign Parts. It provided the family with domestic stability near good schools for the children and was a post he held until his retirement in 1921. The large Montgomery family henceforward split its time between an overcrowded house in Chiswick and holidays at Moville Place in County Donegal in Ireland. The now 13-year-old Bernard and his elder brother Donald were educated as 'day boys' at the academically distinguished St Paul's School at Hammersmith in London. It was a welcome chance for the boys to escape their mother's baleful influence and Montgomery immediately asserted his independence by joining the school's army class without his parents' knowledge, who had hoped he would follow his father's lead and join the church. It was the rebellious 14-year-old Bernard's first real victory over his mother. Unfortunately Bernard did not prove a good student at St Paul's and frequently clashed with authority. Instead of studying, he energetically threw himself into competitive sports, which he thoroughly enjoyed. The diminutive Montgomery, still fiercely independent, self-sufficient and intolerant of authority, displayed clear leadership skills at team sports, but also earned himself the nickname 'Monkey' from his fellow students given his vicious behaviour on the sports field. Only in his final year did Montgomery redouble his academic efforts as the competitive examination for entry into Royal Military Academy Sandhurst loomed.

A youthful Captain Bernard Montgomery and Brigadier-General J. W. Sandilands, the commander of 104th Brigade, during World War I. Montgomery served a hard apprenticeship on the Western Front, holding a succession of staff appointments.

THE MILITARY LIFE, 1906–42

Montgomery entered Sandhurst in January 1907 at the age of 19 without great difficulty, with his entrance results ranking him 72 out of an intake of 170 cadets that year. Gentleman Cadet Montgomery initially did well, in particular demonstrating powers of leadership that earned him rapid promotion to cadet corporal and marked him out to become a colour-sergeant in his company. A fight between his company and another during which the shirt-tails of an unpopular student were set afire, however, nearly ended his military career. Although intended as a prank, the badly burnt victim

was hospitalized and as a result Montgomery, a ringleader, was demoted and threatened with immediate expulsion. Only his mother's personal intervention ensured he remained to complete his studies, though he was made to do a third term at Sandhurst and lost his seniority in the army lists. A chastened and reformed Bernard eventually passed out 36th in his class, although not high enough to get a coveted place to join the Indian Army, which offered better pay and chances for promotion, as he had hoped. It was a bitter disappointment for an impecunious Montgomery and his family.

Montgomery was commissioned as a second lieutenant on 19 September 1908 in the Royal Warwickshire Regiment, a line-infantry regiment, where his wages and private income from his family would just about cover his living expenses. Between 1908 and 1913 Montgomery served with the 1st Battalion at Peshawar in the North-West Frontier Province of British India, qualifying for a foreign service supplement to his pay, where he learned the rudiments of regimental soldiering, especially man management. This young and rather difficult subaltern, still always at odds with authority, did not fit in well with his hard-drinking fellow officers and remained a virtual outsider since his modest income prevented him from fully participating in the polo games, horse racing and women chasing that he characteristically regarded as largely frivolous pursuits. The dour and argumentative Montgomery found that the rules and restrictions of military life largely suited him, and learned with evident enthusiasm all he could about his chosen profession. However, as a teetotaller he also learnt to despise arcane regimental mess traditions, his hard-drinking 'amateur' fellow officers and, on closer acquaintance with it, the Indian Army, whether through jealousy at being turned down or for some other reason it is difficult to judge. The 1st Battalion returned to Shorncliffe in England in 1912, where Montgomery was befriended and encouraged in his studies by an officer recently returned from Staff College at Camberley.

August 1914 saw the outbreak of World War I, a war that was to have a great influence on Montgomery's future life, making him single-minded in pursuit of his chosen profession and imbuing him with an ambition to succeed. Following the outbreak of hostilities, the 1st Battalion set sail for France and was thrown into battle at Le Cateau on 26 August 1914 at the end of the retreat from Mons. It suffered heavily, with half of its men killed or captured, and the 26-year-old Lieutenant Montgomery, with a group of other survivors, only evaded capture by hiding by day and marching by night back to British lines.

The 1st Battalion was committed again during the first battle of Ypres in October 1914. While leading his company, as a newly promoted captain, during an attack at Meteren on 13 October 1914, Montgomery was shot through the right lung by a German sniper. Although a member of his platoon quickly dressed Montgomery's serious chest wound, his saviour was killed almost immediately. Fortunately for Montgomery, his body provided makeshift shelter that saved his life while he lay out all afternoon unattended. Even so, Montgomery sustained a further bullet wound in the knee. Although so gravely wounded that a grave was dug for him, Montgomery survived his injuries. He was promoted and awarded the Distinguished Service Order for his exemplary courage and gallant leadership.

The debilitating nature of Montgomery's chest wound – leaving him short of breath for the rest of his life and averse to anyone smoking cigarettes nearby – meant he held a succession of staff appointments instead of returning to his regiment for the rest of the war; this undoubtedly saved his life. Following four months' recuperation, in February 1915 Montgomery was appointed a brigade major to the 104th Brigade, part of Kitchener's all-volunteer New Army that was organizing, equipping and training in Lancashire. It was a demanding new job, and as the only regular officer with combat experience Montgomery played an important part in its administration and training.

The 104th Brigade deployed to France in January 1916 and took part in the grinding battle of the Somme. It was a steep learning curve for the young Monty, who learned about the importance of prior preparation and planning, maintaining high morale and implementing new tactical methods if attacks were to be made successfully. By virtue of his sheer drive, capacity for hard work and analytical ability he was steadily promoted and given more demanding staff appointments. Montgomery was appointed the GSO2 (General Staff Officer, Grade 2) of 33rd Division at the beginning of 1917 and in July became the GSO2 (Training) of IX Corps, forming part of General Herbert Plumer's Second Army. Montgomery learnt much from Second Army's approach to trench warfare, whose GOC concentrated on making limited attacks against specific and realizable objectives, made only after meticulous prior preparation and planning. As GSO2 (Training) Montgomery excelled and was given responsibility for running IX Corps' battle-training regime, and he was instrumental in producing a detailed training manual, improving training methods and in conducting rehearsals that enabled his corps to achieve its objectives with minimum casualties.

From 1917 onwards Montgomery became increasingly critical of the British high command and its fighting methods, after seeing at first hand vast numbers of lives being lost with little visible result. In October 1917 Montgomery became GSO2 (Operations) at IX Corps, responsible for issuing all operations orders, and held this appointment through the hard-fought battles of the Lys and Chemin-des-Dames. The 30-year-old Montgomery was promoted to the rank of lieutenant-colonel on 16 July 1918 and became chief of staff of 47th (London) Division, commanded by General G. F. Gorringe, who largely left responsibility for running the division to him, including the issuing of directions for offensive operations and training. This experience made Montgomery quickly realize the value of the chief of staff position, as well as the vital importance of simplicity and clarity of planning, a clear purpose and a professional approach to soldiering. It left him convinced that a high standard of training was paramount and Montgomery continued to write outstanding training manuals, synthesising recent experience of modern warfare on the Western Front. In October 1918 his division took part in the final pursuit of the defeated German Army as it conducted a fighting withdrawal eastwards.

The inter-war period

Lieutenant-Colonel Montgomery was posted to the British Army of the Rhine on 24 March 1919, as the British Army transitioned back to peacetime soldiering. Between September and November 1919 Montgomery briefly commanded the 17th Royal Fusiliers. A fervent desire to attend Staff College in 1920 ended in failure, however, until Montgomery secured the assistance of Field Marshal Sir William Robertson, who ensured that his name was added to the list. At Camberley, Montgomery threw himself into his studies with enthusiasm, with his unbridled criticism of current military thought marking him out from his fellow students. Indeed, a combination of his dedication to study and his intolerance made him unpopular. Monty established a close friendship, however, with one of the directing staff – Alan Brooke – whose intellect, sheer professionalism and ability mirrored his own.

Montgomery graduated from Staff College in December 1920 and served as brigade major of 17th Infantry Brigade at Cork in Ireland, engaged in

Lieutenant-Colonel Bernard Montgomery and the officers of the 17th Battalion The Royal Fusiliers at Duren in the Ruhr, autumn 1919. Montgomery briefly served in the army of occupation before securing a coveted place at the Staff College at Camberley.

combating the Irish Rebellion. For this young Anglo-Irish officer this bitter experience of guerrilla warfare against fellow Irishmen provided much food for thought, and he gained a reputation for exemplary efficiency as a staff officer. In 1923 Montgomery was posted as a GSO2 to 49th Territorial Division in Yorkshire, where he established a friendship with Francis de Guingand and further refined his ideas about training, especially that of part-time soldiers. Following a brief stint with his battalion as a company commander, Major (brevet Lieutenant-Colonel) Montgomery was appointed in January 1926 a member of the directing staff of the Staff College at Camberley. It was a fulfilling time for Montgomery, who taught alongside Alan Brooke and Bernard Paget.

Montgomery fell in love and eventually married the fun-loving, affectionate and outgoing Betty Carver on 27 July 1927, although some sceptics saw it merely as a necessary step for a man wedded to his career to secure further advancement in the Army. An Army widow with two sons, whose husband had died at Gallipoli, Betty, a professional artist, could have hardly been more different to Montgomery, having a wide range of bohemian friends completely outside of her husband's experience. Opposites clearly attracted, and Betty welcomed Montgomery's efforts to organize her and her sons' lives. The contrast between the kind, loving and giving Betty and his previous experience of women during his childhood could hardly have been more marked. It was the beginning of probably the happiest period of Montgomery's personal life, with his wife bearing him a son – David.

Montgomery and his wife began the peripatetic life of a military family when he was given the command of 1st Royal Warwickshire Regiment in January 1931, which served in Palestine in 1931, Egypt in 1931–33 and India in 1933–34. Following this appointment, Montgomery served as a senior instructor at the Staff College at Quetta between 1934 and 1937, during which time he clarified his developing ideas about leadership, tactics, man management and modern warfare in general. With Betty's influence softening some of the worst aspects of Montgomery's character and making him a far more amenable colleague than ever before, Montgomery prospered.

Montgomery was promoted to the rank of brigadier and placed in command of 9th Infantry Brigade in May 1937, stationed in Portsmouth. During a series of exercises on Salisbury Plain, Monty tried out on the ground a series of new tactical and training methods he had devised. A personal tragedy overwhelmed his small family in 1937, however, when, following an insect bite while on holiday at Burnham-on-Sea, Betty fell seriously ill and eventually had to have her leg amputated. On 19 October 1937 she tragically died from septicaemia in Monty's arms while he read her the 23rd Psalm. It was a hammer blow for Montgomery from which he never really fully recovered, and it left him lonely and emotionally impoverished for the rest of his life.

The bitter and distraught Monty reverted to type, becoming the self-contained, solitary and unlikeable individual he had been before he met Betty. To assuage his grief Montgomery single-mindedly funnelled his energies and undoubted ability back into his work and dedicated himself to his professional advancement and mastery of the art of war.

Under his command his infantry brigade carried out a series of exercises, including a joint services operation on Slapton Sands, ever mindful of approaching war; as a result of this Monty attracted favourable attention from General Archibald Wavell as a clear forward thinker and trainer of troops. An incident in 1938, however, nearly wrecked his military career. To raise funds for a brigade welfare fund he rented out a garrison football field to the local council. When the enraged War Office found out that military property had been used without its consent it demanded that the money be repaid, but it had already been spent. Monty survived only when it was proved that the funds had been used for a good purpose.

Lieutenant-General Bernard Law Montgomery with his only son, David, in 1941.

In 1938 Montgomery was appointed GOC 8th Division in the British mandate in northern Palestine, engaged in suppressing the Arab Revolt, as a stepping stone to taking command of 3rd Division in the UK. While at the same time training his men for the future war with ruthless efficiency, he went about hunting down and destroying Arab gangs that ranged across the countryside, and in doing so secured relative peace. In April 1939 Montgomery was summoned home, but suddenly fell so seriously ill with pleurisy and suspected tuberculosis that it was believed he would never exercise command again. It appeared that only by sheer willpower did he make a near-complete recovery while aboard ship to England, and by the time he attended a medical board in London he was declared fully recovered.

Major-General Montgomery unofficially took over command of 3rd Division in August 1939 while its current GOC (Major-General Bernard) was away on leave. With part-mobilization already implemented, however, Major-General Bernard was still slated to take this division to France. Following protests and string-pulling by the GOC Southern Army, Lieutenant-General Sir Alan Brooke, Montgomery officially took command of 3rd Division on 28 August 1939. He immediately set about training this formation with a will.

World War II

Montgomery led the 3rd Division – nicknamed the Iron Division – when it went overseas in October 1939 as part of the British Expeditionary Force (BEF), and took up position along the Franco-Belgian border. A series of withdrawal exercises practising all-arms operations by day

and night were carried out under his command during the bitter winter of 1939–40, which later stood the division in good stead. A characteristically outspoken gaffe in a frank and descriptive written order about controlling venereal disease in his division, however, once again nearly cost him his command.

The 3rd Division, under Montgomery's capable leadership, performed extremely well following the German invasion on 10 May 1940, carrying out the advance to the Dyle and the ensuing withdrawal to Dunkirk with great professionalism. Montgomery brought 3rd Division home with only minimal casualties, and briefly commanded II Corps after Brooke was ordered home on the beach at Dunkirk.

Montgomery was highly critical of how Lord Gort had commanded the BEF when he returned to the UK, and his outspoken utterances aroused considerable enmity amongst senior officers. Initially he retained 3rd Division but in July 1940 was promoted to command V Corps, where with considerable relish he put into practice his well-developed ideas on the importance of physical fitness, training and morale. A similar regime was put in place when Montgomery took over XII Corps on 27 April 1941, where he immediately embarked on another clean sweep of the overaged, unfit and lame. In the process, however, Montgomery caused considerable jealousy and he fell out with the outgoing commander, Lieutenant-General Claude Auchinleck, the new GOC Southern Command, beginning a lasting feud between the two men. In November 1941 Montgomery was appointed GOC Southern Command, and he immediately implemented intensive training for offensive operations.

Lieutenant-Colonel Bernard Montgomery while commanding officer of 1st Battalion The Royal Warwickshire Regiment. This unit served in Palestine, Egypt and India while under his command during what was probably the happiest period of his life.

THE HOURS OF DESTINY

Montgomery, Eighth Army and El Alamein

Montgomery's 'hour of destiny' came in August 1942 when he assumed command of Eighth Army in North Africa. Between 1940 and 1942 the Western Desert had witnessed pitched fighting between Axis and British Commonwealth troops as fighting see-sawed backwards and forwards along the Mediterranean littoral. Following the disastrous battle of Gazala in May and the fall of Tobruk in June 1942, the victorious Axis armies, commanded by Generalfeldmarschall Erwin Rommel, surged forwards across the Egyptian frontier. Under the personal command of General Sir Claude Auchinleck, the Commander-in-Chief Middle East and de facto GOC Eighth Army (following the sacking of its previous incumbent), the battered Eighth Army had halted Panzerarmee Afrika during the so-called first battle of El Alamein. With both sides exhausted, Eighth Army went on the defensive and began rehearsing plans for meeting a renewed German attack. It began the much-needed process of resting, reorganizing and retraining its troops for a future clash of arms.

Eighth Army had already learnt much from bitter experience about waging war in the desert, but was still arguably in the doldrums following the first battle of El Alamein. Although initially heralded as a victory, realization quickly spread that it had done little more than temporarily halt the first Axis offensive towards the Nile Delta, and after two years of desert fighting, Eighth Army was back at the start line where it had begun in 1940. The writing was on the wall for General Sir Claude Auchinleck, who had already lost Churchill's confidence by wisely insisting that his tired army was incapable of resuming the offensive until mid-September. Churchill wanted a 'winning' general.

The initial choice of a new Commander-in-Chief, Middle East and GOC Eighth Army fell respectively on Lieutenant-General Sir Harold Alexander and Lieutenant-General William 'Strafer' Gott. Unfortunately the ill-fated Gott was killed in an air crash returning to Cairo. General Sir Alan Brooke, the Chief of the Imperial General Staff (CIGS), finally convinced Churchill to accept as his protégé the 54-year-old Lieutenant-General Montgomery as the new GOC Eighth Army. To many it appeared a strange choice since Montgomery was a virtual unknown outside military circles.

Montgomery decisively took command of Eighth Army on the evening of 13 August 1942, two days before he was due to do so, and with characteristic self confidence, determination and vigour immediately set about imposing his

The 7th Battalion The Suffolk Regiment being inspected by General Bernard Montgomery, commanding V Corps, at Sandbanks in Dorset, 22 March 1941. Following Dunkirk, Montgomery put into practice his deeply held ideas on training and 'binging up' troops while holding successive commands.

will on Eighth Army. It was the crowning point of his career and an opportunity to put all his long-developed ideas about leadership, training and doctrine into practice by recreating Eighth Army in his own image, although as recent research shows in many respects he owed much to the foundations laid by his predecessor.

The decisive Montgomery immediately exerted a strong 'grip' on his staff and injected a much-needed breath of fresh air, demonstrating from the outset his incisiveness, determination and will to succeed. He immediately galvanized his headquarters staff and senior officers into activity and challenged the endemic atmosphere of doubt and defeatism that pervaded. The headquarters staff underwent an immediate shake-up. Brigadier Francis de Guingand, Auchinleck's former BGS (Brigadier, General Staff), was appointed as Montgomery's chief of staff, who henceforward coordinated all staff functions and freed Monty to think and plan. A new joint army–air headquarters was created to facilitate cooperation between the two services co-located at a healthier location on the coast near Burgh el Arab, with a smaller tactical headquarters created from where Monty would direct the battle. No more 'bellyaching' or questioning of orders was tolerated – officers were to carry out orders and no spurious arguments were to be presented against doing so. With characteristic ruthlessness Montgomery immediately replaced unsuitable, out-of-touch or overage officers judged unfit for the task with men he had already identified, knew and trusted.

The Western Desert was virtually unknown to Lieutenant-General Bernard Montgomery when he arrived in Cairo to take command of the badly battered Eighth Army in August 1942. It was a task, however, he embraced with characteristic self-confidence, determination and relish.

General Sir Harold Alexander, Prime Minister Winston Churchill and the newly appointed Lieutenant-General Bernard Montgomery, GOC Eighth Army, in the Western Desert, 19 August 1942. In only a short period of time Montgomery played a major role in improving the morale and combat effectiveness of Eighth Army.

Lieutenant-General Brian Horrocks, for example, was brought in to command XIII Corps.

The presence of its new commander was immediately felt from top to bottom of Eighth Army when Montgomery, full of self-confidence, immediately projected his personality by issuing new orders to his subordinates in an attempt to distance himself from his predecessor, which were based on his new appreciation of the situation. Eighth Army would stand and fight where it stood, brooking no further withdrawal. Further reinforcements were immediately ordered up from Cairo and definite instructions, already partially prepared, dictated that the vital Alam Halfa Ridge was to be held in strength by bringing up 44th Division from the Nile Delta.

The shaken morale of much of Eighth Army particularly worried Montgomery – with many officers and men badly lacking confidence because of a prior lack of overall firm direction. They suffered a 'Rommel complex' and many were openly distrustful of their weapons and equipment. Suspicion between the arms of service was widespread and many were sceptical of the Desert Air Force's ability to give promised support to the army. To rebuild morale and 'binge up' Eighth Army for the battle ahead, Montgomery immediately toured his new units and formations and at deliberately informal meetings introduced himself and explained the purpose for which Eighth Army was fighting, how he would win and the part that would be played by each ordinary soldier in defeating Rommel. These carefully stage-managed talks proved highly successful in spreading his new 'gospel' of victory and convincing his men to believe in and identify with him. To help stress the difference between himself and his predecessors Monty acquired an Australian

Above: Brigadier Francis de Guingand, Monty's long-serving chief of staff, stands on the front steps of the GOC Eighth Army's caravan near Tripoli, 1 February 1943. As well as being an accomplished staff officer, de Guingand proved a gifted diplomat and on numerous occasions smoothed relations between Montgomery and Eisenhower and other senior officers.

Right: Lieutenant-General Bernard Montgomery watches the developing battle of El Alamein from the turret of his Grant command tank, 5 November 1942. Montgomery always maintained a strong 'grip' on his subordinates to ensure that his 'master plan' was carried out.

bush hat on which he proudly displayed the cap badges of units under his command. Such acts of showmanship proved highly effective and quickly won the trust, loyalty, devotion and confidence of his men, who were quickly convinced that he was interested in them, understood their needs and had a formula for victory that could be achieved with relatively little loss of life.

In Monty's view Eighth Army needed major changes in organization and an overhaul of its fighting methods, which were already in the process of being altered. A series of organizational changes were immediately implemented, including the formation of a new *corps de chasse*, commanded by Lieutenant-General Lumsden, from armoured units withdrawn from the front line. Further experimentation in organization was banned. Henceforward the GOC directed that divisions would fight as complete formations under their commanders with clear-cut tasks and definite objectives, rather than going into action fragmented into brigades and small battle groups as before.

The new GOC proved himself a commander sufficiently willing, ruthless and confident enough in his own judgement to impose his own carefully thought-out interpretation of doctrine on his subordinates, and ensure that realistic training was carried out based upon it. In particular the new GOC rammed home the vital importance of concentration and successful combined-arms operations as a prerequisite of success, as well as far closer cooperation with the Desert Air Force. With Montgomery's backing, the already ongoing process of developing methods of centralizing the control of artillery and employing it en masse gathered pace.

The entire Eighth Army badly needed training at all levels and in turn divisions began to be pulled out of the line to carry out intensive individual and collective training in the formations in which they would fight, to ensure that current doctrine permeated throughout formations. Live ammunition was freely employed to give added realism. Training carried out stressed the cooperation of all arms and close air–ground cooperation. Repeated rehearsals of major operations of war were carried out, especially those required in the forthcoming offensive, with particular emphasis placed on gapping minefields.

The battle of Alam Halfa

The new GOC Eighth Army oversaw in a very short space of time a remarkable transformation in his forces, with a new confidence, *esprit de corps* and sense of professionalism spreading throughout its ranks. Following a visit on 19 August an astonished General Sir Alan Brooke observed: 'I knew my Monty pretty well by then but I must confess I was dumbfounded by the situation facing him, the rapidity with which he had grasped the essentials, the clarity of the plan.'

Lieutenant-General Bernard Montgomery, the GOC Eighth Army, standing in front of his personal Grant command tank, 5 November 1942. This AFV (armoured fighting vehicle) provided him with relative safety during visits to the headquarters of front-line formations and units in the Western Desert.

Eighth Army had not completed its reorganization or training programme, however, before the Axis mounted their long-awaited full-scale offensive towards Cairo. The Axis attack began on the night of 30–31 August when Panzerarmee Afrika advanced on the southern flank of the El Alamein position, though it was immediately delayed by minefields, dogged British resistance and Allied air power, which dominated the battlefield. The German armour quickly ground to a halt in front of the massed anti-tank guns, tanks and artillery dug in on the Alam Halfa Ridge, which Monty had correctly assessed as a key position. Under repeated massed aerial attack and artillery fire, Rommel bowed to the inevitable and on 2 September the Axis forces withdrew behind the minefields largely unmolested. This defensive victory was a huge fillip to Eighth Army's morale and inspired great confidence in Montgomery's generalship. The German offensive had occurred just where Monty had predicted, had been fought according to his plan and Eighth Army had defeated it in detail. Although extremely cautious throughout and especially during what was a very limited pursuit, owing to Montgomery's recognition of just how blunt Eighth Army still remained as an offensive weapon, the battle was a striking vindication of his leadership, justified his efforts to introduce new fighting methods and was the first unequivocal British victory of the Desert War.

Montgomery immediately insisted, as had his predecessor, that Eighth Army would not attack until it was ready, with its troops properly trained and equipped, and not unless it possessed an overwhelming superiority in numbers and *matériel*. Efforts redoubled during this operational pause to prepare Eighth Army for a future offensive as soon as the dust settled. A programme of intensive training for offensive operations was rolled out, with each formation practising the tasks assigned to it according to the developing plan. As an example, X Corps practised how to gap deep minefields, with special reference paid to neutralizing enemy anti-tank screens with massed artillery. A large quantity of new personnel and modern equipment – anti-tank guns, artillery and particularly Sherman tanks – was issued to armoured units.

The battle of Alam Halfa

This illustration shows an 6-pdr anti-tank gun, crewed by the hard-pressed 1st Battalion The Rifles Brigade, busily firing at German tanks at the climactic moment of the engagement on 31 August 1942. This element of 22nd Armoured Brigade defended an area of low and broken ground at the foot of the Alam Halfa Ridge. The engagement began when Grant tanks belonging to the 3rd/4th City of London Yeomanry, dug in on the upper slopes, opened fire when the advancing enemy approached to within 1,000m. Within minutes, 12 Grants were 'brewed up' by German Mk IV Specials. The dug-in anti-tank guns held their fire until the advancing tanks were within a few hundred metres and then quickly destroyed 19 of them, although several gun positions were overrun. The now-disorganized enemy attack was finally halted by a defensive artillery barrage, and, just as the light failed, a counter-attack by the Royal Scots Greys forced them to withdraw.

A 25-pdr opens fire during the opening barrage of the second battle of El Alamein, 23 October 1942. The numerically superior British artillery, handled with considerable tactical flexibility and en masse, proved to be a battle-winning weapon.

Little was left to chance, with each phase of the planned offensive carefully planned, stage-managed and rehearsed.

The second battle of El Alamein

The renewed and reinvigorated 195,000-strong Eighth Army was a very different fighting machine in terms of its morale, scales of modern equipment and combat effectiveness by mid-October 1942, following the root-and-branch changes Montgomery had overseen since he assumed command. By late October it was equipped with 1,038 tanks, including significant numbers of modern Shermans and Grants. A large number of new 6-pdr and older 2-pdr anti-tank guns were in the hands of the infantry, moreover, and an impressive artillery park had been created. Supplies were plentiful; vast quantities of fuel and ammunition were available from stocks held in the delta. The overall state of training, however, was still below that which Montgomery believed was necessary to defeat a much better-trained Axis Army, especially in terms of combined-arms operations and inter-service cooperation.

Montgomery applied his clear thinking to the problem of breaching the formidable Axis defences at El Alamein and defeating Rommel's Panzerarmee in detail, building upon the work of his predecessor, while at the same time minimizing the risk of another humiliating defeat. The nature of the El Alamein position, with the German defences anchored on the coast in the north and the impassable Qattara Depression in the south, compelled him to make a frontal attack. The clear and simple final plan for Eighth Army's offensive at El Alamein – dubbed Operation *Lightfoot* – bore all of Montgomery's hallmarks, being a meticulously planned and prepared set-piece battle reminiscent in some respects of World War I. It was based on his careful appreciation of the strengths and weaknesses of Eighth Army and the sheer strength of the German defences that confronted it. Eighth Army would employ its overwhelming advantage in infantry, armour, artillery and air power in a frontal attack to penetrate the Axis defences, built in great depth and protected by deep minefields, and offset acknowledged German tactical prowess on the battlefield. Eighth Army would make a series of alternate thrusts that would grind Panzerarmee Afrika down in a battle of attrition, while maintaining balance itself, before launching a breakthrough employing a large armoured reserve.

XXX Corps would break the crust of the German defences during the initial night attack and then force a passage through the deep main Axis defences in the north, while XIII Corps mounted a subsidiary attack in the south. The initial attacks by XXX Corps – made at night by four infantry divisions supported by a massive artillery bombardment and aerial support – would clear

paths through the extensive Axis minefields, through which two armoured divisions from X Corps would advance as soon as two corridors were cleared of mines. As soon as the enemy minefields were cleared by XXX Corps, X Corps would position itself astride the German supply lines to draw enemy armour reserves onto the awaiting British tanks and anti-tank guns. So-called 'crumbling operations' on either side of the breach meanwhile would widen the hole and grind down the enemy infantry. To convince German commanders that the attack in the south was the main British effort, a carefully planned deception scheme was implemented.

Operation *Lightfoot* – began on the night of 23 October 1942 with an artillery bombardment of Axis artillery positions and then front-line defences on a scale and intensity never seen before during the Desert War. A rolling barrage preceded the four divisions of advancing infantry of XXX Corps as they crossed no man's land on a 16km front and entered the Axis minefields. Overhead the Desert Air Force provided protection from air attack and neutralized enemy artillery batteries. Although the advance towards the initial objective – the Oxalic Line – was initially successful, a combination of stiffening resistance and mounting casualties slowed the advance and in turn hampered efforts to clear the Axis minefields. Even so it had been a successful 12 hours with most divisions through the minefields, and some troops had reached the Miteirya Ridge. Unfortunately the work of X Corps' mine-clearance teams was badly delayed due to pockets of enemy resistance, who failed to clear and mark passages through the minefields that night. Although a few corridors were operational by dawn, immense traffic jams built up at the eastern end of the routes. The upshot was that by daylight neither division of X Corps was in a position to exploit XXX Corps' penetration and in place to meet the expected German counter-attacks. The few tanks that reached the Miteirya Ridge were subjected to intense fire from the intact main German defences and forced back into hull-down positions on the reverse slopes.

Further south, XII Corps experienced similar problems when it attacked, and 7th Armoured Division, supported by 51st Division, was delayed by fierce resistance and encountered the same problem when breaching the minefields.

A line of British tanks on the move during the battle of El Alamein, October 1942. Eighth Army possessed considerable numbers of tanks by the time the battle began, including the highly capable US Sherman which outclassed most Axis AFVs.

Only the first of two dense minefields had been penetrated before dawn, though the attack had had the desired effect of confusing the enemy.

The preliminary attacks by XXX Corps on 23 October gave Montgomery, watching the developing battle from his tactical headquarters, considerable grounds for optimism as news filtered in. Although X Corps did not have as many tanks forward as planned, progress had been made all along the front. If the bridgeheads could be strengthened as planned he hoped crumbling attacks would still provoke the German armoured divisions in reserve into making an attack. The morning of 24 October 1942 was marked, however, by chaos and confusion as six British formations, with X Corps superimposed on XXX Corps, tried to clear routes for their vehicles and push forward into the bridgeheads created in the Axis defences. The overall progress actually made by Eighth Army's further advances on 24 October, however, proved extremely disappointing, with few tanks penetrating the minefields and little ground being gained by the infantry in local attacks. Despite repeated urgings from Montgomery and Leese, little effort was made by the GOC 10th Armoured Division to move his tanks forward and across the Miteirya Ridge. A night attack by 10th Armoured Division, supported by a massive bombardment, became mired in a minefield, took heavy losses to air attack and failed to gain ground, to Monty's extreme annoyance that his orders had again been disobeyed. A combination of blunt speaking and a threat to remove commanders who disobeyed orders appeared to have the desired effect, but it was discovered next morning that the armour had still not reached the forward slopes of either Miteirya Ridge or Kidney Ridge as planned. In the south, moreover, 7th Armoured Division's attack was called off due to enemy resistance and difficulty in getting through the minefields.

The failure of X Corps' half-hearted attacks and the general poor performance of the armour on the night of 24–25 October showed that

General Montgomery, GOC Eighth Army, looks at a map spread out over the bonnet of his jeep, Italy, 30 September 1943. He spent a considerable part of each day visiting his subordinates in their forward headquarters.

Battle of El Alamein, October–November 1942

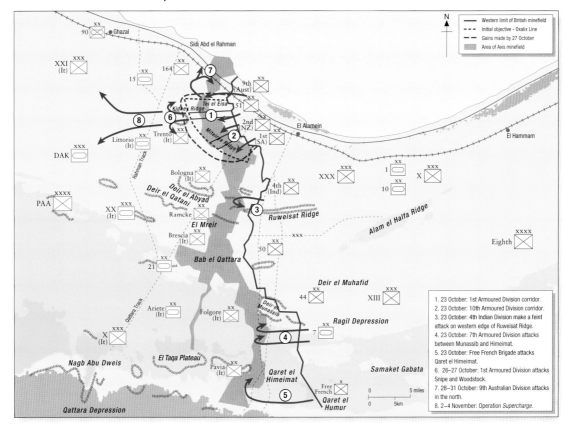

Operation *Lightfoot* was clearly not going according to plan, though XXX Corps had mostly reached its objectives. A combination of these factors and mounting losses compelled a hurried rethink by Montgomery, who quickly adopted a different approach of making consecutive thrusts in different sectors of the front line to grind down enemy armoured reserves until nothing was left to oppose a massive armoured thrust. To secure surprise, seize the initiative and avoid a stalemate a new line of attack was chosen with 1st Armoured Division forming a protective shield for 9th Australian Division, which would begin crumbling operations northwards towards the coast. Meanwhile, XXX Corps would defend the Miteirya Ridge while 10th Armoured Division would be withdrawn into reserve. Little progress was made anywhere the following day, although attacks by XII Corps tied 21. Panzer-Division and the Italian 132[a] Divisione Corazzata 'Ariete' down in the south.

On 25 October 1st Armoured Division made little progress against powerful anti-tank defences. Further attacks by XXII Corps in the south that day also made little ground, but did fix enemy armoured reserves in the area.

The Australian attack on the night of 25–26 October towards Point 29, a small rise dominating that part of the battlefield, however, was a complete success, while 51st Highland Division made ground towards its original Oxalic objectives. The newly arrived Rommel reacted by throwing in more and more tanks in small-scale counter-attacks involving 15. Panzer-Division, 164. leichte-Division and the Italian XX Corpo, which had little effect other than grinding down his reserves and using up valuable fuel. The 90. leichte-Division was also brought into the area, fulfilling the aim of Montgomery's strategy by forcing Rommel to commit more and more reserves in meeting Eighth Army's small-scale attacks.

The Australians renewed their attack northwards on 28–29 October. While preparations were under way other formations continued their attacks towards Kidney Ridge or the Oxalic Line. Both the New Zealand Division and 9th Armoured Brigade were withdrawn into reserve. The 1st Armoured Division successfully drew enemy reserves upon itself as it advanced from the northern corridor, whose full-scale armoured counter-attacks were broken up with considerable loss.

Montgomery shifted the weight of his attacks northwards when 9th Australian Division exerted further intense pressure towards the coastal road on the night of 28–29 October, with good gains initially being made. Although stopped short of its final objective, the desired heavy losses were inflicted on units of 26. Panzer-Division and 90. leichte-Division. The 15. Panzer-Division and later elements of 21. Panzer-Division transferred from the south were also drawn into this dogfight, which by virtue of superior numbers and *matériel* Monty knew he would win. The successes achieved in this section briefly led Monty to contemplate attempting breakthrough in this area. Further heavy fighting continued on 30 October as the Australians established a salient across the road and railway line. It convinced Rommel that this attack would be followed by Eighth Army's main blow and he withdrew 21. Panzer-Division into reserve.

The breakout

Montgomery had changed his mind about where to make his breakthrough attempt, however, with the British main effort now directed south of the Australian salient. The new plan – dubbed Operation *Supercharge* – bore similarity to Operation *Lightfoot*, with XXX Corps' infantry attacking in

A column of German and Italian prisoners taken during the opening phases of the battle of El Alamein march into captivity, 24 October 1942. Eighth Army took large numbers of Axis POWs as morale in Panzerarmee Afrika steadily slipped away.

strength at night from near Point 29 followed by massed armour. It was supported by massed artillery fire and attacks from the Desert Air Force. A subsidiary attack, meanwhile, by XIII Corps in the south would hopefully mislead the enemy about the real direction of the attack.

The reinforced New Zealand Division led the main attack on 2 November, with 9th Armoured Brigade following close behind the advancing 151st and 152nd Infantry Brigades. It made rapid progress and achieved all its objectives with minimal losses. On either flank neighbouring divisions simultaneously carried out crumbling attacks on the Axis defences. As planned 9th Armoured Brigade passed through, advancing behind a rolling barrage, and overran the enemy defences around the Rahman Track, despite suffering heavy losses to a German anti-tank screen. The enemy defences had been cracked open. The 1st Armoured Division rushed forward into the battle, but was halted by tanks and anti-tank guns albeit at heavy cost to the defenders. Further British attacks elsewhere caused the Axis line to buckle steadily as the defenders neared the point of collapse. Meanwhile, 9th Australian Division also successfully advanced to the north as realization spread that enemy resistance was slackening.

The end was in sight for Panzerarmee Afrika by mid afternoon on 3 November. Under heavy pressure Rommel took the difficult decision to withdraw XX Corpo and XXI Corpo behind the Deutsches Afrikakorps (DAK). Hopes for an orderly withdrawal, however, were dashed upon receipt of a 'stand and fight' order from Hitler, and Rommel reversed his own orders. The battle of attrition had swung Eighth Army's way by early morning on 4 November, with early attacks encountering only minor opposition from an opponent near collapse and steadily withdrawing from the battle. With further organized resistance impossible, a beaten Rommel authorized a withdrawal of his remaining troops from El Alamein.

The Axis forces, however, were spared a *coup de grâce*, by what can only be described as a lacklustre pursuit by Eighth Army. A combination of Montgomery's failure to organize an effective pursuit, traffic congestion and later rain allowed the Panzerarmee to slip away along the Via Balbia, albeit leaving behind its infantry, all of whom were destined for POW camps.

Conclusion

The decisive victory achieved at El Alamein was a personal triumph for Montgomery and for all the officers and men of Eighth Army. It had not been achieved without cost, however, with Eighth Army suffering 13,560 men killed, wounded or missing during ten days of pitched fighting. Almost overnight Montgomery became front-page news and a public hero as a result of a brilliant debut on the battlefield. Montgomery's inspirational leadership, self-confidence and sheer professionalism had been instrumental in improving the morale and combat effectiveness of Eighth Army and turning around its fortunes at Alam Halfa and then at the second battle of El Alamein. An important caveat must be made that Monty had profited on his arrival in North Africa from his predecessor's work and that Eighth Army as an organization had already made great strides in improving its combat effectiveness and planning to meet a German offensive at Alam Halfa. It was something that Montgomery, anxious to make own his stamp upon Eighth Army at the time, could not admit. Indeed, as a 'new broom' Monty deliberately distanced himself from his predecessor and continued to do so in his post-war writings.

The incisive plan for the battle of El Alamein, showing in meticulous detail how the enemy was to be fought, and his masterful conduct of the fighting itself was testimony to Montgomery's intelligence and professionalism, a result of years of dedicated study of modern warfare, and his assessment of the capabilities of the troops under his command. The operational techniques employed in making an attack on the formidable German defences deliberately pitted British strengths – armour, artillery and air power – against German weaknesses. The set-piece battle of attrition that Montgomery devised and then fought with characteristic self-confidence, determination, skill and ruthlessness had gradually worn down Axis strength and morale to breaking point. The essence of his approach at El Alamein had been to keep Axis commanders unbalanced and constantly guessing where the next thrust would fall; he did this by always keeping reserves on hand, retaining flexibility and by using his superior mobility to shift his attacks from area to area. The battle did not play out entirely in keeping with his master plan, however, as he later disingenuously claimed it had. Indeed, Montgomery demonstrated considerable flexibility on the battlefield when setbacks occurred. The failure of an armoured breakthrough on the second night of the battle led Montgomery to adopt a different approach, making consecutive thrusts in different sectors to ground down enemy armoured reserves until nothing was left to oppose a massive armoured thrust. His conduct of the battle had not been free of mistakes either, with the superimposition of X Corps on XXX Corps during its early phase resulting in command-and-control problems, as well as causing considerable congestion and confusion near the Miteirya Ridge.

Tac HQ – Tactical Headquarters

This illustration depicts Montgomery's tactical headquarters during Eighth Army's advance on Tripoli, with the three heavily camouflaged caravans used as his sleeping quarters, map room and office forming a backdrop. It shows Montgomery chatting with two key members of his personal staff: Brigadier Francis de Guingand, his long-serving chief of staff, and Brigadier Bill Williams, his chief of intelligence. Behind Montgomery stands his long-serving batman – Corporal English – who is holding two cups of tea for the visitors. The group is completed by two long-serving aides-de-camp – Captain Johnny Henderson, 12th Royal Lancers, and Captain John Poston MC, 11th Hussars (wearing his unit's distinctive headgear), who served with Monty from El Alamein onwards. Unfortunately Captain John Poston MC was tragically killed while serving as one of Montgomery's picked liaison officers only days before the end of the war in Europe when his jeep was ambushed in northern Germany. His death was a great personal blow to Montgomery, who wept openly at his funeral.

Montgomery, Operation *Overlord* and the battle for Normandy

Monty's appointment in December 1943 as GOC British 21st Army Group and as temporary Allied Land Forces commander under the overall command of General Dwight D. Eisenhower of all US and British troops destined for the long-awaited invasion of Northwest Europe began his second 'hour of destiny'. Following the controversies surrounding the invasion of Sicily and the frustrations of the ill-thought-out Italian campaign, it brought Monty back to the centre of activity. Although clearly saddened by leaving Eighth Army, Montgomery was supremely confident in his own ability and willingly shouldered the burdens of his new appointment, fearing a repetition of many of the mistakes made in mounting the invasion of Sicily. Indeed, many of his worst fears about Operation *Overlord* were confirmed when Churchill showed him an outline of the existing invasion plan at Marrakesh in December 1943.

Lieutenant-General Montgomery, accompanied by key highly qualified members of his personal retinue including Major-General Francis de Guingand as his chief of staff, with characteristic drive, determination and brimming with self-confidence immediately gripped his new command the day after he arrived in the UK, radiating the same authority and professionalism as he had to Eighth Army in the desert to all he met in London. It was the beginning of what was arguably his greatest performance of the war. The 'hidebound' staff of 21st Army Group was purged, albeit on a far more restricted scale than in Egypt owing to fewer suitable replacements being available and Monty's awareness of the sensitivities of the home army, and known and trusted new men were appointed to key command and staff appointments. On 11 January he addressed his staff and two days later his designated commanders, setting out his working methods for winning battles and warning that all bellyaching must cease.

Montgomery worked wonders in immediately dispelling the cloud of uncertainty and indecision that to date had enveloped Operation *Overlord*.

A smiling British soldier gives German POWs taken during the battle of El Alamein a cheeky victory sign. Large numbers of Axis troops without water had little option other than to surrender following the battle as they lacked motor transport.

He held his first conference on 3 January where the existing plans developed by General Frederick Morgan and his COSSAC (Chief of Staff, Supreme Allied Commander) headquarters staff for the invasion of Normandy were reviewed with his characteristic incisiveness and clarity of mind. Monty enjoyed virtually a free hand in developing a new plan for *Overlord*, with Eisenhower delegating to him full responsibility for planning the invasion and entrusting land operations to him. Indeed, relations between Monty and Eisenhower were extremely cordial, with each left free to get on with their own work. Within days the existing plan for a landing of three divisions on a 37km-wide front was recast for fear that immense confusion would result and that the Germans would easily seal off and destroy a bridgehead. Despite consternation and resentment in some quarters, the size of the initial landing in Normandy was increased to five divisions, spread across an 80km-wide bridgehead between the river Orne and the Cotentin Peninsula, with airborne landings by three divisions on either flank. An increase in the number of landing beaches, moreover, allowed follow-up formations to land far more quickly than envisaged before and build up supplies before the Germans could mass reinforcements in the invasion area. The Anglo-Canadian Second Army, commanded by General Sir Miles Dempsey, would land on the left and the First US Army, commanded by General Omar Bradley, on the right flank of the invasion area. On 21 January Eisenhower gave his approval for this clear, simple and well thought-out revised plan, although finding the necessary assault landing craft led to a postponement of the invasion.

Monty, having provided an outline plan and delegated the necessary authority, left de Guingand and his competent staff to work out the details during the spring and early summer, with the planning of the highly complex assault landing demanding most attention. A detailed outline plan for the ensuing build-up of forces, the expansion of the bridgehead to include the Cotentin Peninsula by US forces and preparations to meet an eventual German counter-attack was also developed in detail, with the British and Canadians landing in eastern Normandy and the American forces to the west. The early capture of Caen by the British Second Army, a vital communications centre located near an area of high ground and terrain suitable for building forward airfields, was a prerequisite for an advance southwards across the Caen–Falaise plain and an eventual breakthrough

British infantry wade ashore during the invasion of Sicily in July 1943. Montgomery helped plan and then lead Eighth Army during Operation *Husky*.

towards Paris. This industrial city would act as a pivot for Second Army, which would shield the First US Army engaged in seizing the Cotentin Peninsula, capturing the vitally needed port of Cherbourg and establishing its own part of the front line protecting the initial lodgement running from Villers-Bocage to Avranches. The First US Army and Third US Army, after it became operational, would then break out southwards from St Lô into Brittany to seize further ports and the Loire. With its flanks secure, the Allied force

would then advance eastwards towards Paris on a broad front. The dissemination of a map by Montgomery laying down a series of phase lines indicating the anticipated steady advance of Allied troops over a period of time, however, proved to be a serious mistake. It became a hostage to fortune and gave rise to considerable controversy after the fighting bogged down about exactly what Monty really intended to do in Normandy and how far operations had stuck to his master plan. Stiff resistance was expected from Rommel and the Westheer (Western Army), with intelligence correctly assessing fierce fighting on the beaches and anticipating that spirited counter-attacks would immediately be made against the bridgehead by local reserves.

Monty was also deeply concerned about the morale and fighting efficiency of the US and British troops destined for D-Day. As he had before El Alamein, Montgomery devoted considerable time and effort to improving morale. A whirlwind tour was carried out throughout the UK by Montgomery during the spring and early summer of 1944, during which he visited units and formations destined for D-Day. During informal (albeit carefully stage-managed) meetings Monty introduced himself to his fighting troops. Using a carefully prepared speech, he succeeded in gaining their trust and confidence, instilling a belief in themselves and the plan and 'binging them up' to fight the Germans. Visits were also made to factory workers, dockers and railway men to bolster flagging civilian morale and fully exploiting his status as a national hero. These visits proved to be a resounding success, raising the confidence of the troops in their leader and bolstering the flagging public morale.

Monty also strenuously endeavoured to improve the combat effectiveness and level of training of the British and US formations destined for Normandy, although the latter were left to their own devices in terms of doctrine. Monty tried to spread the lessons learnt by Eighth Army in combat by holding a series of conferences for senior officers as well as bringing home experienced formations, although the Home Army had already done much to assimilate the perceived lessons of North Africa. Monty made a major contribution to improving tactical effectiveness by insisting that all formations in 21st Army Group followed a standard interpretation of operational doctrine. Intensive individual and collective training was carried out during which the importance of tank–infantry cooperation, battle procedure, the employment of artillery and tactical cooperation with aircraft was driven home. A series of large- and small-scale realistic exercises were also held across the UK, practising combined-arms training, amphibious landings and other operations of war.

Supreme Headquarters, Allied Expeditionary Force (SHAEF) meets in London, 1 February 1944. Montgomery played a key part in the planning phase of Operation *Overlord* by completely overhauling the existing plan and widening the scope of the initial D-Day landings.

Normandy landings on D-Day, 6 June 1944

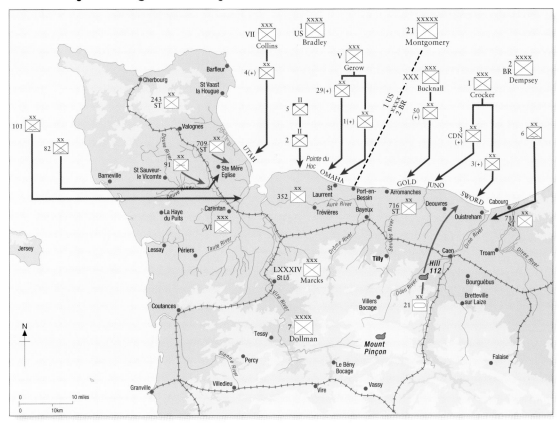

The Normandy campaign

The D-Day landings on 6 June 1944 – arguably the greatest set-piece battle of Montgomery's career – proved resoundingly successful, with large numbers of Allied troops ashore by the end of the day. It was not, however, without its setbacks. The heavy casualties suffered by US troops at Omaha Beach initially gave serious cause for concern, while later that day Anglo-Canadian troops failed to secure the full planned extent of the bridgehead and fierce counter-attacks by 21. Panzer-Division meant that Caen eluded capture. Overall though the successful D-Day landing was a stunning tribute to Montgomery's leadership, foresight and professionalism during its planning.

The ensuing battle for Normandy proved to be a long, drawn-out and bloody affair, with Montgomery remaining in operational control of all Allied land forces. It was arguably the most testing time of Montgomery's long military career, during which his generalship was placed under greater scrutiny than ever before.

Montgomery maintained a characteristically firm 'grip' on the developing operations in Normandy to ensure that 21st Army Group followed his 'master plan'. Montgomery closely supervised the Anglo-Canadian Second Army, commanded by Lieutenant-General Miles Dempsey, throughout the battle, but he largely gave Lieutenant-General Omar Bradley's First US Army a free rein

American troops wade ashore in Normandy on 6 June 1944. The US forces suffered heavy losses on Omaha Beach at the hands of the alert German 352. Infanterie-Division, who fought with great tenacity and held up the initial assault for some time.

apart from broadly suggesting how operations should develop in the Cotentin Peninsula and southwards towards St Lô. The battle for Normandy was conducted by Montgomery from a small tactical headquarters at Creully (later relocated to Bray) from D-Day+2. Each morning Montgomery met formation and unit commanders at their headquarters to discuss the current situation, and issued directions for future operations. A small staff of carefully picked young liaison officers roamed the battlefield acting as Montgomery's 'eyes and ears', busily apprising him of the developing battle. Further information was obtained by the Phantom service, eavesdropping on his subordinates' radio nets.

The early operations in Normandy went largely to plan as the initial Allied lodgements were linked into an 80km-long bridgehead and as the build-up of fresh troops and supplies over the beaches continued largely without interference. The failure to take Caen on D-Day and the rebuff of 7th Armoured Division's attempts to outflank the city at Villers-Bocage on 13 June represented a major setback to Montgomery's initial 'master plan', although as a matter of principle he refused to admit openly that anything had gone wrong. In a striking demonstration of his strategic flexibility, the failure to capture Caen compelled Montgomery to rethink and develop a new plan, although in many respects it only involved a change in emphasis. While still wanting to capture Caen at the earliest opportunity, Monty henceforward emphasized that attracting the German armoured reserves onto Second Army (acting as a hinge on the left flank of the bridgehead) was the key to success, and that by doing so it would facilitate First US Army's operations towards Cherbourg and its later eventual breakout from Normandy. Unfortunately, Monty would not admit to his US allies that the failure to take Caen had resulted in a change of plan, with Eisenhower firmly convinced that a breakthrough at Caen was imminent. This misunderstanding about Second Army's primary role now being to fix and wear down German armoured reserves, rather than achieve a specific objective, nearly proved fatal to Montgomery, and caused his operational methods to be placed under close scrutiny.

Montgomery came under growing pressure from mid-June from politicians, Eisenhower, the staff at SHAEF and the US and British press to achieve results, despite the fact that German resistance had rapidly increased. The apparently disappointing results of a long series of Anglo-Canadian attacks during June, the failure to break through at Caen and the ponderous manner in which these attacks were carried out, as casualties mounted, exposed Montgomery to particular criticism about the way the campaign was developing and led to accusations that he was being overly cautious.

These accusations had some basis in fact. Monty indeed did display caution operationally during a series of ponderous pitched battles fought in and around Caen by Second Army. He did this in order to fulfil his new strategy, reflecting his fundamental concern with keeping 21st Army Group balanced with strong reserves and on a sound administrative

A group of heavily laden British troops from 3rd Division assemble on Queen Red Beach, part of Sword Beach, at 0830hrs during the D-Day landings. Overall the initial landings on D-Day proved a great success and only encountered limited German resistance.

basis. The mounting casualties suffered by Second Army, the natural defensibility of the bocage and the impressive strength of the German front-line defences prompted Montgomery to mount set-piece offensives in future. The ensuing attacks on the German defences in and around the ruins of Caen – Operations *Epsom*, *Charnwood* and *Goodwood* – broadly followed the same lines, with the operational methods employed by Montgomery and his subordinates an amalgam of pre-war doctrine and lessons learnt from operations, including El Alamein. These set-piece attacks on each occasion were carried out on a narrow front and in great depth, with overwhelming artillery, naval gunfire and air power deployed to maximum effect in support of the advancing infantry in order to destroy the German defences, instead of pitting dwindling British manpower in battle against the Wehrmacht. A lengthy period of time was required to plan each operation in meticulous detail, as well as to amass sufficient supplies and bring forward reinforcements.

The first large-scale British offensive directed at Caen – Operation *Epsom* – began on 26 June after being delayed for four days by atrocious weather and the resulting slow arrival of fresh troops, ammunition and supplies. The attack by the newly arrived British VIII Corps, commanded by Lieutenant-General Richard O'Connor, on 26 June took place on a narrow front – 6.5km wide – towards and then across the river Odon between Carpiquet airfield and Villers-Bocage. Around 600 artillery pieces supported it, together with naval gunfire. The advancing infantry, denied full air support by poor weather, suffered heavily at the hands of 12. SS-Panzer-Division and the Panzer-Lehr-Division before the abortive offensive was halted five days later in the face of heavy German counter-attacks having failed to reach its objectives at the cost of 4,020 casualties. Although achieving only negligible territorial gain, the slogging match had succeeded, however, in inflicting heavy enemy losses and drawing in the available German armoured reserves.

The underlying reasons behind Montgomery's cautious approach displayed during Operation *Epsom* were straightforward, being dictated throughout

The headquarters of the 4th Special Service Brigade arrives from several LCIs (Landing Craft, Infantry) at Nan Red sector on Juno Beach on D-Day. The commandos played a key role in the D-Day landings and then fought on alongside regular units in the front line in a conventional role.

the Normandy campaign by his acute awareness of German fighting prowess and the strengths and weaknesses of the Anglo-Canadian troops at his disposal. By June 1944 the British Army was a wasted asset, with its manpower reserves nearing exhaustion, and Montgomery always fought with a close eye on casualty conservation and the maintenance of fragile British morale. This restricted his freedom of manoeuvre and scope of operations. As the campaign progressed and casualties mounted this problem was exacerbated, with even greater reliance placed on air power, artillery and armour in later attacks (assets that Monty possessed in comparative abundance) to grind down the Westheer.

The growing appearance of a stalemate in Normandy and mounting Allied casualties during bitter fighting in the bocage and around Caen in late June and early July 1944 caused growing criticism of Montgomery's leadership from Eisenhower, senior Allied officers at SHAEF and from officers at 1st US Army, as well as the US and UK press, who were clamouring for success. He was accused of being overly cautious and of failing to secure a much-promised breakout from the Normandy bridgehead. A group of highly critical senior British soldiers and airmen at SHAEF, who already had an axe to grind with Montgomery because of his heavy-handed treatment of them before D-Day, and the failure to secure promised airfields near Caen, displayed particular venom towards him. In particular Air Chief Marshal Tedder (the Deputy

D-Day landings, 6 June 1944

The successful Allied landings in Normandy on 6 June 1944 owed much to Montgomery, who had turned the existing flawed plans into a practicable operation for war and improved the morale and overall combat effectiveness of Allied troops.

This illustration depicts officers and men of No. 4 Commando disgorging from an LCA (Landing Craft, Assault) on the extreme left of Queen Red Beach, during the initial assault on Sword Beach. This elite unit, with two attached French troops from No. 10 (Inter-Allied) Commando, was tasked with neutralizing key enemy defensive positions at the casino at Riva Bella and then a gun battery at Ouistreham. Following a brief hold-up, No. 4 Commando fought its way off the beach and onto the lateral road running behind the waterfront. The French Commandos led the advance into Ouistreham before successfully capturing the Casino strongpoint assisted by a Sherman DD tank. The men of No. 4 Commando assaulted the heavily fortified gun battery at the mouth of the river Orne as planned, but withdrew after discovering that the gun emplacements were empty.

Montgomery briefs his British and US liaison officers at his tactical headquarters near Osnabrück before they depart on their daily visits to front-line formations, 12 April 1945. These hand-picked young officers provided the 'Master' with a reliable and up-to-date source of information about the developing battle.

Supreme Commander, directing beneath Eisenhower) proved an implacable opponent who openly pressed for Montgomery's resignation. Although Brooke sent over emissaries from London to pour oil on troubled waters, SHAEF failed to dampen down its criticism.

The ruins of Caen formed the focal point of British efforts in Normandy in early July, although the fighting proved indecisive yet again. Second Army began a further deliberate assault – Operation *Charnwood* – on Caen on 8 July using I Corps, comprising three infantry divisions and a supporting armoured brigade, with massed artillery, tactical air power and RAF strategic bombers paving the way for advancing infantry and tanks in a devastating attack on the city. Following fierce fighting, primarily against I SS-Panzerkorps, the ruins of Caen north of the river Odon fell on 9 July at the cost of 3,500 casualties and 80 destroyed tanks. Not all of the city, however, was in Allied hands.

Montgomery doggedly pursued his strategy of drawing the German armoured reserves upon Second Army without being deflected by this failure and the resulting mounting criticism. During early July operations were mounted along the river Odon and preparations began for another set-piece offensive near Caen, originally intended to immediately precede a 1st US Army offensive towards St Lô. Indeed, Monty remained characteristically self-confident, optimistic and bullish. A combination of pride, hubris and a pathological unwillingness to admit weakness meant that Monty remained adamant that all was going to plan.

The Anglo-Canadian Second Army launched Operation *Goodwood* on 18 July, with the intention of bringing the German armour massed near Caen to battle, securing the remaining part of the ruined town and advancing onto the Bourgebus Ridge beyond. It was the largest British offensive to date, involving three corps. The initial advance by VII Corps' armoured divisions was preceded by massive saturation bombing by strategic bombers, followed by an attack employing 750 Allied tanks to break the German line, outflank Caen and advance into good tank country south of the city towards the Caen–Falaise road. Having failed to break through and after heavy losses the operation was terminated on 21 July with the loss of around 440 tanks and 5,000 casualties. Although partially successful in clearing the rest of Caen, the massed armour was brought to a grinding halt before Bourgebus Ridge by the in-depth German defences, which inflicted crippling losses in tanks, and by torrential rain that deluged the battlefield.

The failure of Operation *Goodwood* – the single most controversial episode in the battle of Normandy – led to a furious outburst of disapproval from the US press and at SHAEF, largely because of Monty's unwise and overly optimistic statements to war correspondents and his communications with Eisenhower that made it appear that an all-out armoured breakthrough was imminent. Although he may well have believed great success was possible, such pronouncements proved to be a huge mistake on Monty's behalf. When the attack failed to deliver results, Eisenhower, supported by Tedder, wanted him sacked. Although badly angered, Eisenhower showed considerable restraint by choosing to leave Montgomery in command. He voiced his disappointment by exhorting to Montgomery that the time for caution was over. To compound matters Monty unwisely also tried to bar Churchill, himself growing critical of Montgomery's command, from visiting him at his tactical headquarters in Normandy. It was arguably the most dangerous point in Montgomery's military career, raising the real prospect of his being sacked. Only Brooke's intervention and flight to Normandy, where he virtually dictated an apologetic letter for Montgomery to write, saved his protégé from being sacked. When Churchill visited Blay on 20 July a charming Montgomery convinced him that the campaign was still going to plan.

The crisis in command revolving around Montgomery's leadership was largely forgotten, however, when the long-delayed US breakout from Normandy – Operation *Cobra* – finally got under way. The initial attack on 25 July, coinciding with another by the newly operational First Canadian Army down the Caen–Falaise road on the British front, began with the saturation bombing of the Panzer-Lehr-Division and powerful attacks on a narrow front by VIII and VII Corps. On 27 July 2nd Armoured Division broke into open country, encountering steadily diminishing German resistance. The almost complete absence of German armoured reserves in the American sector was a striking vindication of the strategy employed by Montgomery (they were still engaged against 21st Army Group). On 30–31 July the US VIII Corps captured Avranches at the base of the Cotentin Peninsula.

The successful US breakout into the Brittany peninsula and then eastwards by Lieutenant-General George S. Patton's newly operational Third Army towards the Seine, threatening to outflank the remaining German forces in Normandy tied up opposing the Anglo-Canadians, was the crowning achievement

Three infantrymen from 8th Rifle Brigade advance with extreme caution across open terrain, south-west of Caen in Normandy, June 1944. Heavy and irreplaceable infantry casualties made Montgomery rely more and more on tanks, artillery and air power to win battles.

A 6-pdr anti-tank gun and Sherman tanks in the centre of Caen, 10 July 1944. The population of this industrial town paid a heavy price for their eventual liberation, which after fierce fighting and RAF bombing raids left Caen in ruins.

of Montgomery's generalship in Normandy and a vindication of his much-maligned strategy. It was not achieved, however, without heavy loss of Allied lives, especially 21st Army Group. The extent of the Allied breakthrough and lack of German resistance offered to the Third US Army to a degree caught Monty and US commanders off balance. The ill-judged and unsuccessful German offensive at Mortain, intended to seal off the US breakout, only worsened the situation for the German high command and the retreating elements of Heeresgruppe B (Army Group B) were eventually caught in the Falaise Pocket by advancing British and US troops as the German defence in Normandy crashed into ruins. When the Falaise Pocket finally closed on 22 August 10,000 German troops trapped within were killed and 50,000 were taken prisoner. Those that escaped across the Seine did so without their heavy weapons and equipment.

Conclusion

Montgomery played an instrumental part in the planning and preparation for Operation *Overlord* as GOC 21st Army Group and Allied Land Forces commander, and he probably had as much if not more significance than his later command in France. As General Eisenhower later admitted: 'No one else could have got us across the Channel.' A combination of a new plan and other preparations for the battle ahead transformed a risky assault landing into a practicable operation of war. The campaign in Normandy ended in a complete and spectacular victory for Monty for which he deserves much credit. It left the Westheer a shattered wreck, incapable of mounting an effective defence within the borders of France.

Monty's generalship during the battle of Normandy, however, has proved highly controversial, something that can be traced back to his own egotistical insistence that everything had gone to plan. This had not been the case. The initial failure to secure Caen resulted in far greater emphasis being placed on drawing upon the British Second Army the German armoured reserves and allowing the First US Army to eventually break out against minimal opposition. Monty followed his personal doctrine in Normandy of unbalancing his opponent while remaining balanced himself, with feint attacks made all along the line to draw in his German opponents while keeping his own troops concentrated for a massive, overwhelming blow at a weak point. All the while

Montgomery insisted on maintaining balance by keeping reserves in being to carry out the next thrust. Monty's generalship was indeed cautious and certainly did not take risks, but it delivered victory in a cost-effective manner in Normandy, obeying the imperative of minimizing casualties and keeping the morale of Allied troops intact, who loyally stuck by him. These offensives did achieve the objective of drawing upon them the vast majority of German armoured formations. The cautious operational techniques he employed were appropriate to the British Army of 1944, on account of its clear strengths and weaknesses that in particular required the careful husbanding of infantry and in its place employing an abundance of *matériel* whenever possible.

The Normandy campaign exposed Monty's marked weakness as a coalition general, especially his inability to communicate with his peers and his often-patronizing tone towards US generals. The atmosphere of mutual trust and confidence that had characterized relations between Monty and his US Allies during early 1944 quickly evaporated as a hoped-for early breakout failed to materialize and the fighting bogged down in Normandy. Indeed, Monty won the Normandy campaign only at considerable personal cost in terms of the confidence that Eisenhower, American commanders and senior British officers at SHAEF placed in him. To an extent he was lucky to retain his command.

Lieutenant-General Montgomery introduces Prime Minister Winston Churchill to his new puppy 'Rommel' at his tactical headquarters at Creully in Normandy, 7 August 1944. A serious clash between the two men was only narrowly averted by the intervention of Major-General Francis de Guingand.

Montgomery, Operation *Market Garden* and the Battle of the Bulge, September 1944 to January 1945

The late autumn and winter of 1944 was not a time of destiny for Montgomery in the sense of achieving further notable success on the battlefield, though under his command the Anglo-Canadian 21st Army Group advanced rapidly through northern France and into the Low Countries. The speed and scale of the German collapse and the inability of the shattered Westheer to mount an effective resistance, apart from isolated garrisons occupying the Channel ports, raised widespread expectations that the end of the war was in sight. For Montgomery the ensuing campaign in Northwest Europe was a time of acute frustration and one that starkly outlined some of the serious limitations of his leadership, personality and generalship as part of an Allied coalition.

The month of September did not begin well for Montgomery, with the appointment of Eisenhower on 1 September 1944 as overall operational commander of Allied ground forces, as well as Supreme Commander Allied Expeditionary Force, after SHAEF's headquarters became operational in France. Although up to the last minute the egotistical Monty remained convinced he would remain in command, this long-planned and awaited change in command was not a surprise. Monty now commanded 21st Army Group only. To assuage his hurt *amour-propre*, as a consolation prize Monty was simultaneously appointed to the rank of field marshal, though as GOC of the Anglo-Canadian 21st Army Group he held a command of equal status with the US commanders of 12th Army Group and 6th Army Group, who were lower in rank. To rub salt into his wounds the US invented the rank of 'general of the army' for Eisenhower in order to make him equal in status with Montgomery.

The relations between Eisenhower and Montgomery remained poor at best. Indeed, the existing animosity between them dating from the battle of Normandy steadily worsened between August and September 1944 over Allied leadership and strategy, which at times threatened inter-Allied cooperation as support coalesced along largely national lines. An obsessed Montgomery was highly critical of Eisenhower's suitability as Allied ground forces commander given his lack of experience commanding fighting troops, and pressed for him to be replaced. Indeed, the characteristically egocentric Montgomery still fervently believed he was far better qualified in training and experience for the appointment, although he was prepared to serve under Lieutenant-General Omar Bradley, whom he knew and respected as a field commander in recognition of growing US preponderance in France. An increasingly divisive and fundamental disagreement over future strategy and the best means of quickly winning the campaign in Northwest Europe as Allied forces crossed over the river Seine, however, ensured that Eisenhower and Montgomery remained permanently at loggerheads, although they both periodically papered over the widening cracks between them. Eisenhower championed an advance by two widely separated army groups, each under its own commander, which respectively would move north and south of the Ardennes on a broad front through France towards Germany. The diametrically opposed Montgomery, supported by Field Marshal Alan Brooke (the CIGS), championed the case of a concentrated advance on a single line by two army groups, under his own command, consisting of 40 fully supplied divisions drawn from 21st and 12th Army Groups that would sweep the remnants of the Westheer before its irresistible weight and would together drive north past the Ardennes, take the Ruhr in its stride and culminate with the capture of Berlin. Although an impressive idea on paper, when it was first aired 40 divisions had not yet even landed in France and supplies were extremely limited.

Eisenhower, with the US President, US Joint Chiefs of Staff, SHAEF and US public opinion behind him, was in a virtually unassailable position on both counts, but he was also extremely reluctant to sack Montgomery given his prestige, his British press support and the need to maintain Allied unity. The US commander, always keen on consensus

A seated Lieutenant-General Montgomery plays with his two pet dogs, 'Hitler' and 'Rommel', at tactical headquarters in Normandy, 6 July 1944. The small menagerie of pets he kept provided Montgomery with a source of much-needed relaxation.

and compromise, initially proved more receptive to Montgomery's ideas than anticipated, giving 21st Army Group priority in supplies, since clearing the Channel ports and capturing V1 launch sites in the Pas-de-Calais were temporarily administrative and political priorities. The divisive debate over Allied command and strategy, however, was by no means over. With dogged persistence Montgomery returned again and again to the attack, and the argument dragged on until well past the Battle of the Bulge, demonstrating Montgomery's political *naïveté* and failure to accept that political considerations outweighed military ones. It had a serious effect on personal relations between key Allied commanders and on inter-Allied relations in general, with Monty failing to accept that his idea was dead both politically and militarily. He failed to understand the key facts: the political impossibility of placing a British general in charge of numerically preponderant US troops, the increasing reticence of senior US officers to serve under British command and the inherent dangers of mounting a single offensive into Germany. Montgomery's autocratic style of command, personal arrogance and bullying manner as he tried to cajole Eisenhower into changing his mind only reinforced American hostility.

Operation *Market Garden*

The sense of euphoria and widespread belief that the end of the war in sight may well have caused Montgomery to make the most serious mistake of his military career in September 1944: Operation *Market Garden*. Indeed, Montgomery's preoccupation with getting a Rhine bridgehead and administering a fatal knockout blow to Nazi Germany diverted his attention from realizing the logistical significance of Antwerp and its approaches and preventing the escape of the German 15. Armee.

The employment of airborne forces in support of 21st Army Group's advance north of the Seine was discussed on several occasions during August 1944, but the speed and success of its pell-mell advance led to the abandonment of these plans each time. When Eisenhower placed First Allied Airborne Army in support of 21st Army Group on 4 September, Montgomery decided to employ it during the next stage of the advance from Antwerp to pave a way for an armoured advance over the Maas and the Rhine that would bypass enemy resistance, outflank the Siegfried Line and end with 21st Army Group poised to launch a decisive thrust across the north German plain. An element of Montgomery's thinking at the time may well have been that if he could force a Rhine crossing Eisenhower would have to give 21st Army Group priority for supplies and force his hand into accepting his 'single thrust' strategy north of the

During the opening phase of Operation *Market Garden*, C-47 Dakotas drop members of 1st Airborne Division near Oosterbeek. The distance separating the initial drop zones and the objective meant that only one battalion reached the road bridge in Arnhem.

Men of the 1st Parachute Regiment take refuge in a shell hole outside Arnhem during Operation *Market Garden*. The 1st Airborne Division was heavily engaged by elements of II SS-Panzerkorps, which was refitting nearby following its mauling in Normandy.

Ruhr. Indecision initially reigned over whether Wesel or Arnhem would be a suitable objective. On 10 September Montgomery decided on seizing a bridgehead over the Lower Rhine at Arnhem instead of at the more lightly defended Wesel, and deferred clearing the Scheldt Estuary. Later that day Monty met with Eisenhower who, following a highly charged discussion about command and strategy, endorsed Montgomery's plan to secure a Rhine bridgehead, granted permission to postpone clearing the Scheldt and allocated 21st Army Group the necessary supplies to carry it out.

The start date for Operation *Market Garden* was fixed for 17 September 1944 and detailed (albeit rushed) planning, fundamentally flawed by poor liaison between the air and ground components, immediately began in England for the initial airborne drop, while Dempsey and Horrocks planned the ground link-up. First Allied Airborne Army would assist Second Army in making a rapid 160km armoured thrust from the Meuse–Escaut Canal northwards towards Nunspect on the Zuider Zee. Second Army would then turn eastwards into Germany across the north German plain. The plan involved I Airborne Corps parachuting in during daylight and capturing bridges over successive canals and rivers near or in towns en route – Eindhoven, Nijmegen and Arnhem – providing a carpet through enemy territory over which British armour would advance. The US 101st Airborne Division would seize the bridges near Eindhoven, the US 82nd Airborne Division the bridges and commanding terrain near Nijmegen and 1st Airborne Division the final road and railway bridges over the Lower Rhine at Arnhem after landing on heathland west of the town. Then, XXX Corps would advance up a single two-lane road, initially leading across flat and open sandy terrain and later water-logged polder that would make cross-country movement (if required) extremely difficult, to relieve each airborne division in turn. It was an ambitious plan and a timetable for an advance by XXX Corps was drawn up largely predicated on the limited German opposition that had been experienced since the collapse in Normandy. The limited airlift available, news of growing German troop concentrations and serious misgivings voiced by several participants over the plan failed to deflect a characteristically self-confident, highly optimistic Montgomery, egged on by Browning, as the plan gained a momentum of its own even though casualties were likely to be high.

The initial phase of Operation *Market Garden* that began on 17 September proved partially successful, with XXX Corps successfully relieving the two US airborne divisions. Instead of meeting minimal opposition it was repeatedly held up and delayed en route, however, by heavy German resistance and blown bridges. The ambitious timetable for the advance by XXX Corps slipped accordingly, leaving lightly equipped airborne troops to fight on alone for far longer than anticipated. The unfortunate 1st Airborne Division fared badly when it landed virtually atop II SS-Panzerkorps, which was resting near Arnhem. Fierce fighting raged in and around the town. Although 2nd Battalion the Parachute Regiment seized and held Arnhem Bridge for five days, it surrendered on 21 September with half its number dead or

wounded. The battered remnants of the lightly equipped 1st Airborne Division, left to its own devices following a communications breakdown, were pushed back and trapped in a rapidly contracting pocket near Oosterbeek, where hopes were pinned on the imminent arrival of XXX Corps. Although 1st Airborne Division fought on largely unsupported for several more days the end was in sight. On 26 September its remnants were evacuated across the Lower Rhine to safety.

The highly ambitious Operation *Market Garden* ended in a decisive defeat that had squandered the Allies' strategic reserve and cost 1st Airborne Division

A column of Cromwell tanks, part of the Guards Armoured Division, drives along 'Hell's Highway' towards Nijmegan during Operation *Market Garden*, 20 September 1944. The choice of a single road for the advance by XXX Corps proved to be a major error.

Plan for Operation *Market Garden*, September 1944

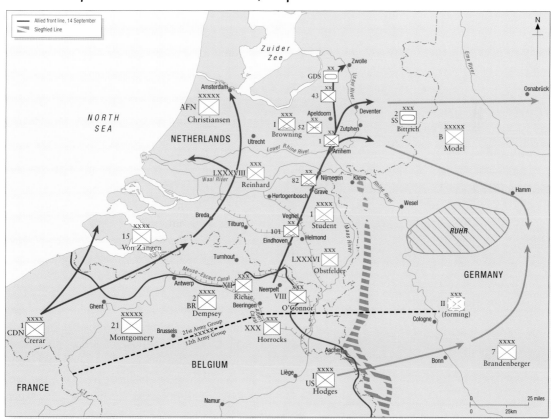

Above: A battle-worn group of British paratroopers advance through the ruins of Oosterbeek on 23 September 1944 during Operation *Market Garden*. By this point battle exhaustion and shortages of ammunition were steadily undermining the combat effectiveness of 1st Airborne Division.

Below: Field Marshal Sir Bernard Montgomery discusses the latest situation with Major-General B. Matthew Ridgeway, the US commander of the 18th Airborne Division, during the Battle of the Bulge.

alone over 1,000 dead and 7,000 POWs. It had been a major error in concept and execution by Montgomery, who had ignored mounting warnings from his staff about increasing enemy strength at Arnhem and shortcomings in what had never been a clear and simple plan. Uncharacteristically for Montgomery, planning and preparation for this offensive had been slapdash from the start. A combination of a poor and overly complex plan, a wilful underestimation of German powers of resistance, the single exposed line of advance, a failure to land airborne troops immediately by the bridge in Arnhem and the use of two separate lifts had cost his reputation dear. The opportunity cost had been high, with Monty's fixation with Operation *Market Garden* arguably prolonging the war by diverting his attention away from the far-more-important clearance of the Scheldt Estuary. With considerable justification Montgomery blamed himself in large part for the failure of the overly ambitious operation. Indeed, his unwavering commitment to the operation may well have been in part to rid himself of the reputation of being overcautious and partly to be the first to get troops across the Rhine. Arnhem proved the only defeat of Monty's long military career and one he disingenuously later claimed as having been 90% successful, having seized the bridges en route as planned. Without the bridge over the Lower Rhine, however, they led nowhere. Although the positions along the highway to Arnhem later proved to be useful jumping-off points for attacks eastwards across the Rhine in March 1945, Second Army was left with a long and indefensible salient throughout the winter.

The Battle of the Bulge

The bleak autumn of 1944 was a time of frustration for Montgomery and of continuing conflict with his US Allies, as the dispute over Allied command and strategy dragged on to Eisenhower's obvious chagrin. Following Arnhem and the costly and unglamorous clearance of the Scheldt Estuary, the front line in Northwest Europe had bogged down in the rain, mud and snow of winter. The euphoria of the summer and early autumn gave way to despondency as another winter at war lay ahead. While the Allies consolidated their position, the Germans had, however, almost miraculously rebuilt and re-equipped their armies and created a strategic reserve from virtually nothing.

The German Ardennes offensive launched at dawn on 16 December 1944 caught the Allies almost completely off guard by the speed and ferocity of the initial assault, as armoured spearheads cut through the weakly held US front

line. With low cloud and fog shielding the advancing tanks of 5. Panzerarmee and 6. SS-Panzerarmee from aerial attack, rapid progress was made through the Ardennes, splitting apart the defending US armies, which suffered heavy casualties and had many men taken prisoner. Initially, confusion reigned supreme over the exact scale and extent of the German offensive. Within five days the Germans had driven a deep 80km-wide wedge between the First US and Third US Armies and had nearly reached the river Meuse, threatening a further advance towards Antwerp.

The German offensive had driven large elements of the First US and Ninth US Armies northwards out of direct control of Bradley's 12th Army Group. On 20 December a shaken Eisenhower ordered Montgomery to take command of the northern side of the bulge, giving him what he had long desired – command of the complete northern sector of the Allied front line. Within hours a characteristically self-confident and energetic Monty visited the badly-shaken and demoralized commanders of the First US and Ninth US Armies – Lieutenant-General Hodges and Lieutenant-General William Simpson respectively – who were immediately 'gripped' and taken under firm control. With information in short supply, liaison officers were immediately dispatched to find out the exact position of the front line, who encouragingly discovered that despite heavy losses two of Hodge's US divisions were successfully withdrawing. To shore up the front line, British troops were placed under Simpson's command, whose own troops took over part of First US Army's front. The headquarters of 21st Army Group quickly redeployed elements of XXX Corps behind Ninth US Army in case of a US collapse, with tanks blocking bridges over the river Meuse. A strategic reserve was quickly formed under the command of Major-General Lawton Collins from part of US VIII Corps and 51st (Highland) Division behind Ninth US Army, with orders to prepare a counter-offensive.

Montgomery, by virtue of his self-confidence, energy and professional ability played a key role in gradually stabilizing the northern front line, reorganizing his command and restoring the morale of his tired and shaken US subordinates during late December, although his refusal to immediately counter-attack the German spearheads until ready and sure of victory attracted US criticism. A tactless and cocksure Monty, however, could not resist the temptation to lord it over his US Allies that he had been right about having a single northern commander and that the current situation was the result of two widely separate thrusts into Germany. By 24 December the threat to Antwerp had receded and the following day Patton's Third Army, advancing from the south, relieved the US 101st Airborne Division in the beleaguered town of Bastogne. A gradual improvement in the weather, moreover, allowed the devastating weight of

A heavily camouflaged sniper, part of 6th Airborne Division, on patrol in the Ardennes on 14 January 1945. Montgomery's command of US forces during the Battle of the Bulge proved highly controversial at the time and relations between him and his US Allies plummeted to new depths.

American soldiers of the 1st US Infantry Division advance towards Faymonville during the final phase of the Battle of the Bulge. The reluctance of Montgomery to counter-attack on the northern side of the bulge was a source of considerable criticism.

Allied air power to dominate the battlefield. The German offensive had clearly petered out, but a characteristically cautious Montgomery was unwilling to advance, to the chagrin of Eisenhower, Patton, Bradley and his own US subordinates, and still hoped that the Germans would put even greater numbers of troops into the exposed salient created by their offensive. Montgomery was also very mindful of the heavy casualties an attack would entail and the need to keep forces in being for an eventual push into Germany. The failure to launch a promised attack on 1 January by Montgomery coinciding with a thrust from the south aroused Eisenhower and his colleagues' ire. Eisenhower's growing resentment of Montgomery was fuelled further by an inflammatory letter warning that failure was imminent unless a change in the command structure was implemented that placed him in command of 21st Army Group and 12th Army Group for an advance on the northern line into the Ruhr. The abortive attack on 1 January, together with this letter, convinced Eisenhower that it was time to rid himself of his difficult subordinate, but was dissuaded from sending the relevant signals by de Guingand, who immediately persuaded a shocked Monty to apologize.

The long-awaited US attack under Montgomery's command on the northern flank of the bulge began on 2 January, with the First US Army advancing south-eastwards towards St Vith and the Third US Army advancing northwards from Bastogne. On 6 January elements of both formations linked hands at Houffalize, bringing an end to the Battle of the Bulge. Although the previous front line was not fully restored until 7 February, the defeated Germans had little option but to withdraw in order to save what they could from a debacle that had cost them 85,000 killed, wounded or taken prisoner and 600 tanks.

Montgomery made an often-overlooked contribution to Allied victory during the Battle of the Bulge. As Allied commander on the northern flank he played an important part in stopping the initial rot and stabilizing the front line. Montgomery became the subject of considerable American criticism however, which focused on his patronizing attitude towards US generals, accusations he had displayed excessive caution and his repeatedly delayed and rather half-hearted offensive from the north, with the US generals who had served under him claiming that the compromise attack at Houffalize had been forced upon them. The full weight of US fury was directed at Montgomery, however, following a press conference on 7 January, which he had hoped would end a 'slanging match' in the British press that had given the unfortunate impression that Montgomery had been called in to sort out a mess of the

US' own creation in the Ardennes. The opposite, however, was the result. A cocksure, self-congratulatory and patronizing Montgomery described in glowing terms to assembled journalists his contribution in first halting the German offensive, stressing the role played by British troops in an 'interesting' battle that had cost thousands of US lives, and gave the unfortunate impression that he had saved the American forces from disaster. Such a tactless, one-sided and inaccurate account of the Battle of the Bulge had the opposite effect Montgomery had hoped for. Unsurprisingly, Eisenhower, Bradley and other US generals involved in the fighting were livid. To compound matters the Germans intercepted an account of the conference being transmitted to London, rewrote it in an even more damning manner and broadcast it disguised as the BBC,

Battle of the Bulge, December 1944 to January 1945

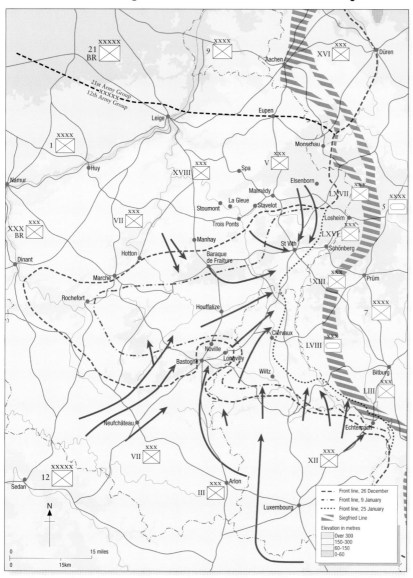

A Universal Carrier lands from a Buffalo amphibious vehicle during the Rhine Crossings, 24 March 1945. This was Montgomery's last set-piece battle of World War II, and he encountered only light resistance.

adding further fuel to the fire. Although Churchill and Brooke did their best to play down the conference, the damage was well and truly done. Although a thick-skinned Monty appeared to think he would retain control of US formations after the Battle of the Bulge ended, he could not have been more wrong. Eisenhower remained fuming with rage and other US generals openly refused to serve under Montgomery. The ultimate price paid by Monty was a complete loss of confidence in him by Eisenhower (who now openly both distrusted and disliked him) and his deeply resentful US Allies, which eventually led to his being sidelined, his strategic ideas and command proposals being ignored and the withdrawal of all US forces – Ninth US Army – from under his command as Allied forces advanced deep into Germany. For the rest of the war 21st Army Group was assigned the relatively unimportant and unglamorous task of advancing into northern Germany and towards Denmark, away from Berlin. If Monty had not still enjoyed the full support of Churchill, Brooke and the vocal British press he would undoubtedly have been sacked.

OPPOSING COMMANDERS

Montgomery fought a succession of Axis commanders during World War II, but his name will be for ever linked with one man – Generalfeldmarschall Erwin Rommel (1891–1944). Dubbed the 'Desert Fox' by his British opponents in North Africa, he was arguably Montgomery's single greatest and most famous German opponent, whose reputation as an inspirational leader, professional soldier and opponent of the Nazi regime survives untarnished to this day. Indeed, the Desert War in the popular imagination has been reduced to an almost personal contest between Rommel and Montgomery.

Erwin Rommel was born on 15 November 1891 at Heidenham, near Ulm in Swabia. In July 1910 he began his military career when he joined Infanterie-Regiment König Wilhelm I (6. Württembergisches) Nr. 124 as an officer cadet. Following attendance at the Kriegsschule (a military academy) at Danzig he was commissioned as a *Leutnant* (first lieutenant) on 27 January 1912. As a young subaltern he served on the Western Front in 1914–15, where he established a reputation as a brave, daring, independent-minded and resourceful junior officer. Although badly wounded on three occasions, he survived to be awarded the Iron Cross, Second and then First Class for bravery in the field. In October 1915 Rommel transferred to the new elite

Württembergisches Gebirgs-Bataillon, in which he served in France, Romania and finally Italy. On 27 November 1916 he married Lucia Mollin, who bore him a single son – Manfred. Rommel again demonstrated his military ability in Romania and in particular Italy. While commanding a battalion on the Italian Front, Rommel distinguished himself during the battle of Caporetto (October–November 1917) by capturing the key position on Monte Mataiur, large numbers of prisoners and 81 guns, which turned the battle into a disaster for the Italians. Rommel was awarded the Pour le Mérite – Imperial Germany's highest award for bravery – and for the rest of the war he served on the general staff.

Rommel remained in the tiny Reichswehr Army following World War I as a regimental officer, instead of joining the general staff, and through sheer ability rose steadily through the ranks. Between 1929 and 1933 he taught at the Infanterieschule at Dresden and on 10 October 1933 Rommel took command of an infantry battalion. He then held a series of instructor posts at training establishments. In 1937 Rommel published a small and influential book – *Infanterie greift an* (*Infantry Attacks*) – based on his professional experiences. It sold well and attracted widespread interest, including that of Adolf Hitler, who had already met Rommel on several occasions, whose mobile headquarters Rommel briefly commanded in 1938. On 23 August 1939 Genaralmajor Rommel was appointed commandant of Adolf Hitler's headquarters battalion, which he led during the early months of World War II. As part of his immediate entourage Hitler became closely acquainted with Rommel, who liked him on a personal level because of his bourgeois background and war record.

Field Marshal Montgomery and General Sir John Burnett Stuart sitting aboard Monty's personal Miles Magister aircraft, 8 March 1945. This small liaison aircraft enabled the GOC 21st Army Group to visit the widely separated formations under his command as the advance into Germany gathered pace.

Rommel took command of 7. Panzer-Division in February 1940 at the age of 48, with Hitler's direct support, much to the surprise and resentment of many senior German officers. He brilliantly distinguished himself during the invasion of France in May 1940. Rommel led from the front and demonstrated a firm understanding of fast-moving armoured warfare, proving to be a daring, bold and flexible commander swift to take advantage of his opponents' mistakes. Under his command the so-called 'Ghost' division performed excellently and Joseph Goebbels ensured that the young, handsome and courageous Rommel was surrounded with a blaze of publicity.

Rommel emerged from the French campaign as a popular hero with a glowing reputation as a gifted armoured commander. Hitler was instrumental in appointing the now Generalleutnant Erwin Rommel as commander of the newly formed Deutsches Afrikakorps, which landed at Tripoli on 12 February 1942, to support the demoralized and defeated Italian Army. Rommel quickly adapted to desert fighting and demonstrated his skill at fast-moving armoured warfare against the poorly led, ill equipped and increasingly demoralized British troops. Although initially ordered to stand on the defensive while the Afrikakorps disembarked, on 24 March 1941 he launched a surprise offensive that drove the British back across Libya, with only the isolated port of Tobruk left under enemy control. Rommel's reputation soared and he was given command of the German–Italian Panzergruppe Afrika in August 1941. During the ensuing fighting that ranged across the Western Desert, Rommel proved himself to be a courageous, decisive, and enterprising commander, who was prepared to take risks, do the unorthodox and ruthlessly take advantage of fleeting opportunities presented by his opponents. Rommel earned himself a fully justified reputation as a chivalrous and humane opponent, moreover, in a 'war without hate'. The increasing awe that the ordinary British soldier accorded the 'Desert Fox' was such that Auchinleck instructed his officers that they should dispel by all necessary means the aura of invincibility surrounding Rommel. Although driven back during Operation *Crusader*, Rommel was in no way defeated.

Rommel's glory days in North Africa began when a spoiling attack launched by the Afrikakorps in January 1942 exceeded all expectations and pushed his surprised opponents back from El Agheila deep into Cyrenaica. It was another demonstration of his unorthodoxy, opportunism and leadership. The battle of Gazala in May 1942 proved his greatest success when he trounced a much larger British Commonwealth Army, occupied prepared defensive positions, seized Tobruk and then pursued his broken opponents to El Alamein in Egypt. It was a spectacular achievement and on 22 June Rommel was promoted to the rank of *Generalfeldmarschall*. A further Axis advance into Egypt was halted in July 1942, however, by a heavily reinforced Eighth Army in fighting that eventually resulted in stalemate.

The battle of Alam Halfa in August–September 1942 was the first encounter between Rommel and Montgomery, when the Axis resumed the offensive on the southern sector of the El Alamein position. By this time Rommel was a sick man after two long and hard years of fighting, however, suffering from fainting fits caused by low blood pressure, an enlarged liver and stomach disorders. Rommel's offensive showed little subtlety or originality, relying on speed and surprise, and had only just enough supplies to enable it to breach the British defences and then encircle and destroy Eighth Army like it had at Gazala. The Axis offensive began on the night of 30–31 August, but a combination of deep minefields, air attacks and stubborn resistance delayed progress, and when the Afrikakorps swung northwards earlier than initially planned it was halted by British troops occupying carefully prepared positions on the Alam Halfa Ridge. Fierce resistance and sustained heavy air attack stopped the Afrikakorps dead in its tracks, and on 2 September Rommel bowed to the inevitable and ordered a gradual fighting withdrawal. The so-called 'six day's race' had been a gamble for Panzerarmee Afrika that did not pay off, with Rommel making the fundamental logistical error of committing his strike force without sufficient fuel. He paid the price accordingly against a new, self-confident and thoroughly professional opponent who had divined the plan and was far better prepared to meet an outflanking attack. Henceforward the Allies enjoyed considerable superiority in *matériel* and were commanded by a general who knew how to use it. A bitterly disappointed Rommel was close to collapse and his doctor ordered him home for at least six weeks' recuperation, though not before he laid down orders for the in-depth defence of the El Alamein position.

Rommel was still on sick leave when Eighth Army launched its awaited set-piece offensive on 23 October 1942, pitting huge *matériel* resources under the command of a general who fully exploited this advantage against the weak and overextended Panzergruppe Afrika. Although Rommel returned immediately, it took him two days to reach his headquarters, by which time the battle was essentially lost. On 26 October he toured the shattered Axis front line and was appalled. With losses soaring the Desert Fox was unable to do more than roll with the punches, with supplies of fuel, ammunition and reinforcements reduced to a trickle. With freedom of manoeuvre denied to him, a static defence remained his only real option interspersed with counter-attacks by his few remaining mobile troops. A planned counter-attack en masse on 26 October to throw the British out of the German defences ground to a halt in the face of heavy air attacks and bombardment by massed artillery. Further counter-attacks against British incursions saw the strength of the Afrikakorps whittled away in a battle of attrition it could ill afford to fight. On 3 November Rommel recognized the inevitable and ordered a withdrawal, but almost immediately it was countermanded by a direct order by Adolf Hitler. On 4 November, after British forces broke through, Rommel ordered a retreat, beginning a rapid decline in relations with Hitler, with only a small remnant of his once-proud army eventually escaping.

The decisive defeat Eighth Army inflicted on Panzergruppe Afrika at El Alamein, and news of the Operation *Torch* landings in Morocco and Algeria on 8 November, convinced Rommel that defeat was inevitable in North Africa. A brilliant 2,250km-long fighting withdrawal was conducted by Rommel along the Mediterranean coast into Tunisia early in 1943, closely pursued by Eighth Army, despite his continued poor health. The over-extended US and French forces in Tunisia provided Rommel with an opportunity to demonstrate his tactical virtuosity while the Eighth Army slowly closed up to the Mareth Line. On 20 February Rommel inflicted a sharp rebuff on US forces at the Kasserine Pass, although this ultimately proved little more than a local success before he returned with his troops to

Montgomery congratulates some of the men who successfully outflanked the Mareth Line in Tunisia. The initial frontal attack on this fortified position went extremely badly, but in a demonstration of his flexibility Montgomery shifted the main effort to his left flank in a wide outflanking manoeuvre which paid dividends.

confront Eighth Army. On 23 February Rommel was given command of Armeegruppe Afrika, consisting of Generaloberst Arnim's 5. Panzerarmee and Generale Giovanni Messe's 1st Italian Army. It proved to be a short-lived appointment. The pressure of months of unremitting hard fighting and pressure from Berlin finally exhausted him. On 9 March he handed over command of Armeegruppe Afrika to Generaloberst Arnim on health grounds and left Africa, never to return.

The battle for Normandy

Rommel survived the Desert War with his military reputation largely intact. The two old adversaries from North Africa faced each other again in 1944, across the English Channel, when Rommel was given responsibility for defending the Atlantic coastline of France and Belgium from the long-awaited Allied invasion. As commander of Heeresgruppe B, Generalfeldmarschall Rommel revitalized efforts to fortify the beaches of Normandy and the Pas-de-Calais. During the spring of 1944 he made repeated tours of the defences, overseeing mine laying, the construction of tank traps and obstacles and the building of fixed defences. A major difference of opinion, however, existed in the German high command about how to defeat an Allied invasion. Keenly aware of the overwhelming strength of Allied naval and air power, massive logistical support and improving US and British capabilities on the battlefield, Rommel favoured a positional defence on the beaches, with immediate local counter-attacks by armoured units held in reserve nearby. In contrast, Generalfeldmarschall Rundstedt, the commander of Oberbefehlshaber West, and General Geyr von Schweppenburg, the commander of 5. Panzerarmee, favoured keeping their armoured formations concentrated inland for a massive counter-attack once the Allies were ashore. It proved to be an academic argument in any event given that the available armoured forces were kept under the command of Oberkommando der Wehrmacht (OKW) and released only on Hitler's personal orders.

Generalfeldmarschall Erwin Rommel, the commander of Heeresgruppe B, inspects the Atlantic Wall during the spring of 1944. Under his command the Germans vastly increased the number of mines, beach obstacles and fortifications in Normandy before the Allied invasion.

Rommel was completely surprised by the Normandy landings on 6 June 1944, still convinced that an invasion would come in the Pas-de-Calais, and as a result of the poor weather had gone home on leave to celebrate his wife's birthday and visit Hitler. Rommel immediately returned to France and reached his headquarters at La Roche-Guyon that evening, having missed the most important day of his career, during which the success or failure of the invasion was decided.

The fierce fighting in Normandy in June–July 1944 was a stern test of Rommel's generalship, with only a small quantity of German armour immediately available to oppose the initial landings and expansion of the

bridgehead. An increasingly pessimistic Rommel immediately tried to seal off and destroy the Allied lodgements until a major counter-attack could be launched, but lacking good intelligence and air support and with his available reserves and supplies delayed and decimated by Allied air power and the French Resistance his efforts were hamstrung. Indeed, with reserves carefully doled out by OKW, strict orders against retreat from Hitler, crippling logistical constraints and above all the devastating influence of Allied air power meant that operational manoeuvre was denied Rommel. Those reinforcements that reached Normandy did so in dribs and drabs and were quickly sucked into the fighting, plugging holes in a cobbled-together front line. Only the defensible bocage and formidable German skill at small-unit tactics enabled Rommel to contain the Allies within a narrow bridgehead.

The static and bitterly fought attritional battles that raged in and around Caen and in the bocage could not have differed more from those that Rommel had fought in North Africa. Rommel performed well under the immense pressure he faced, maximizing the potential of the defenders, reacting with skill, flexibility and imagination to Allied moves and inspiring his immediate subordinates and front-line troops. The German high command in Normandy quickly realized that defeat was inevitable, with the Westheer rapidly wasting away in a battle of attrition in which it simply could not compete. A frustrated Rundstedt and Rommel, denied freedom of manoeuvre, quickly concluded that given overwhelming Allied force the invaders could not be dislodged and that the only realistic course was a withdrawal to the Seine. On 16 June Rommel and Rundstedt met Hitler at Soissons to argue their case for more freedom of action, a withdrawal to more defensible positions and the release of reserves desperately needed to fight a war of manoeuvre inland. Instead, Hitler tied their hands by ordering a rigid defence and a massive counter-attack directed against the bridgehead at Bayeux, which failed ignominiously on 26 June with irreplaceable heavy losses. A further meeting with Hitler on 29 June led to a repetition of his inflexible stand-fast orders and upon their return Rommel and Rundstedt requested a limited withdrawal, to no avail. On 2 July Rundstedt and Schweppenburg were removed from command and two days later the more amenable Feldmarschall Kluge took command. By mid-July Rommel believed that the collapse of the German front line in Normandy was imminent and advised his superior accordingly. On 15 July Rommel met Hitler again and implored him to open peace talks since the battle was as good as lost in Normandy. The Führer abruptly rejected the advice of his once-favourite general; it was to be the last time the two met.

Rommel was spared from witnessing the final German collapse in Normandy. On 17 July 1944 Rommel's staff car was strafed by two RAF Typhoon fighter-bombers on the road between Livarot and Vimoutiers and he was hospitalized with major head wounds.

Rommel's peripheral involvement in the clandestine opposition to Hitler's rule came to light while he was still recovering, following the interrogation of conspirators involved in the abortive July 1944 bomb plot. The 'Court of Military Honour' that examined Rommel's case concluded that he should be expelled in disgrace from the Army and handed over to a *Volksgerichtshof* (People's Court) for trial. On 14 October 1944 two generals acting on Feldmarschall Keitel's orders visited Rommel at his home, however, and offered him the choice of public disgrace at a trial or of committing suicide. Following assurances that his family and personal staff would be protected, Rommel took his own life using a cyanide capsule.

Assessment and comparison

Rommel proved to be a worthy opponent for Montgomery, although the latter always enjoyed massive superiority in *matériel* when the two faced each other in battle. Indeed, he was one of the best battlefield commanders the German Wehrmacht produced during World War II, whose inspiring leadership and marked professionalism was demonstrated at every level of command. The two commanders shared some direct personal similarities, most notably the fact that both were consummate professionals and practitioners of war who had devoted their lives to their military careers, although notably Rommel had not had much staff employment. Both were physically small and compact in appearance and had a single son whom they rarely saw during the war. Rommel and Monty were charismatic leaders who established a close rapport with the troops under their command, carefully fostered morale and never squandered lives needlessly. Each had an acute understanding of the power of the media and surrounded themselves with photographers and journalists. Like Montgomery, Rommel frequently made enemies and many who worked alongside him found him a very difficult colleague. The two men had considerable strength of character, with Rommel willing to bend the truth if necessary, confront hard realities and disobey his superiors, including Hitler if the situation demanded it. Similarly, Rommel was also ruthless with his subordinates, and those that did not measure up to his exacting standards or disagreed with his orders quickly received their marching orders. Both enjoyed powerful patronage during their careers, without which it is unlikely they would have reached high rank.

The differences in their style of leadership on the battlefield and generalship, however, could not have been more marked, with Montgomery always favouring set-piece engagements after lengthy preparation and planning, employing overwhelming air and ground superiority, and Rommel excelling at highly mobile armoured warfare on a logistical shoestring. Rommel was always at his best tactically, employing hard-hitting armoured forces in often risky and hastily improvised operations that demonstrated his flexibility, but which largely eschewed detailed planning and regularly outran his supplies. Rommel made the best of a weak hand dealt to him in Normandy, where he also showed

Lieutenant-General Sir Miles Dempsey briefs Winston Churchill on the situation in Normandy, while Montgomery and Major-General G. Symonds listen nearby, 22 July 1944. Montgomery exercised close command over Dempsey and his other subordinates during the campaign in Northwest Europe.

himself capable of considerable flexibility and improvisation, maximizing the power of his defence by reacting flexibly to Allied moves and inspiring his subordinates. A downside of his approach to command and his lack of staff training, however, was that his subordinates were often effectively abandoned for long periods of time and forced to take decisions on their own authority, logistics were often neglected and in North Africa he apparently did not understand the political context of the war.

INSIDE THE MIND

Field Marshal Bernard Montgomery was a consummate professional in a British Army still dominated by amateurs, but he was in the words of one of his closest colleagues not 'a nice man'. This in itself was not a disqualification for command – many other successful leaders were equally unpleasant on a personal and professional basis. The outward image that Montgomery presented to the world as a calm, self-confident and caring leader helped mask the truth. In reality he was a man whose extremely awkward personality frequently impinged upon how he exercised command on and off the battlefield and affected his ability to form personal and working relationships. The Montgomery that many of his colleagues and superiors throughout his career learnt to dislike was arrogant, boastful and egotistical, as well as being fiercely outspoken, thoroughly conceited and unshakeably convinced of his ability and right to command. He lacked humility and always sought to impose his will on others even if they outranked him. Montgomery frequently displayed jealousy, was dismissive of others and was also an extremely ruthless man who did not tolerate fools or those he considered not up to the mark. These negative aspects of his character cumulatively earned him few friends, made him many enemies and had a serious impact on his career and lasting reputation. A human, lonely and more compassionate side to Montgomery's personality, deliberately kept carefully hidden, was apparent to members of his carefully chosen and trusted small inner circle at his tactical headquarters. To these young officers, part of his 'surrogate' family, the 'Master' could be friendly, amusing, sentimental and charming and inspired an intense feeling of loyalty. Overall Montgomery can be characterized as a complex, deeply flawed and idiosyncratic human being and a profoundly limited individual, whose difficult upbringing, early career and personal life made him his own worst enemy.

The harsh childhood that Montgomery experienced left an indelible mark on him and played a pivotal role in shaping his character, instilling key personality traits and undermining his ability to form meaningful personal and

The GOC 21st Army Group addresses members of the 50th (Northumbrian) Division before awarding several of its members medals for gallantry, 17 July 1944. Montgomery had a gift for oratory and for establishing a close bond between himself and the men under his command.

Field Marshal Sir Alan Brooke, Prime Minister Winston Churchill and Montgomery photographed during a visit to tactical headquarters on 12 June 1944. The succession of visitors Montgomery received provided a welcome diversion for the lonely leader of 21st Army Group.

professional relationships with others. A state of running warfare between him and his young, headstrong and determined mother, who ruled the roost with draconian rules, iron discipline and who frequently meted out corporal punishment, characterized his early years. A lack of maternal love left Montgomery emotionally atrophied and, according to Nigel Hamilton's controversial theory, may have made him a repressed homosexual. Instead of cowing him, Monty emerged from this enduring parental conflict as a rebellious, strong-willed, self-confident and fiercely independent loner who was personally insecure and found it difficult to mix with other family members and to make friends with others of his age and standing. A streak of vindictiveness, petty-mindedness and gross insensitivity, even to those whom he knew and trusted, moreover, was also apparent from an early age. Indeed, the emotionally starved Monty displayed an amazing lack of sensitivity and empathy towards others, always confronted authority and was easily prejudiced against those whom he felt were a threat. A combination of his harsh upbringing and early schooling also instilled within Monty considerable personal drive, confidence in his own ability and an iron-willed determination to succeed in that which interested him – soldiering.

Montgomery's experiences during World War I had a major impact on his still-developing personality. As a junior staff officer Montgomery served a harrowing apprenticeship for command, watching British generals expend human life with such profligacy that it convinced him of the need for change. As a result Monty developed an almost obsessive interest in mastering his chosen profession, as well as studying, finding and developing the means to secure victory with the minimum loss of life. It convinced him of the importance of prior preparation and planning, careful man management, intensive training, frequent rehearsals and the marshalling of overwhelming force at the vital point to win battles with minimal loss of life.

The third major impact on Montgomery's developing character was the tragic death of his wife, whose loving attention helped ameliorate the impact of Monty's childhood on his character. An enduring sense of loss and immediate heartfelt grief had a powerful impact on a crushed Montgomery, who withdrew into himself and then threw himself back into his career with even greater single-minded zeal, studying, writing and preparing for the war he fervently believed was imminent. Without her softening influence, many of his existing unpleasant character traits were exacerbated and, apart from towards a small handful of his peers, it made him an even more difficult, anti-social, graceless and prickly man to deal with.

The key personality traits of self-confidence, decisiveness and sheer ability that Montgomery always exuded stood him in good stead as a leader throughout World War II, especially in 'gripping' new commands and imposing his own will upon them. This was particularly when he was appointed GOC Eighth Army in August 1942 and later as GOC 21st Army Group. Unlike his predecessors, Montgomery had the willpower, drive and personal conviction to impose his own ideas on his troops, and he used these opportunities to put into practice his deeply held ideas on doctrine, training and man management.

Montgomery briefs King George VI on the developing situation in Holland in his map caravan, 13 October 1944. The autumn of 1944 proved a time of disappointment for Montgomery as realization spread that another winter at war lay ahead.

The personal, professional and public adulation showered upon him following the successful battle of El Alamein, however, caused success to go to Montgomery's head. It exacerbated his personal insecurities and magnified many of his unpleasant personality traits. Montgomery's vanity and egotism mushroomed and the final vestiges of his personal modesty were cast overboard, with Montgomery actively courting publicity and openly enjoying his status as a national hero. During the remainder of the war, Montgomery became increasingly brash, insubordinate and downright rude to his superiors. Montgomery's abrasiveness and lack of empathy became increasingly problematic when it caused acute personality problems and rifts within the Allied high command, especially since an egotistical Montgomery remained convinced that his ability as a commander was far superior to that of his US Allies. Indeed, many US generals bridled at his overweening self-confidence, arrogance and boastfulness. In particular his relations with Eisenhower sharply deteriorated, with Montgomery never seeming to be able to accept the answer 'no' until it reached the point where he was nearly sacked. As Field Marshal Sir Alan Brooke, the CIGS, later wrote: 'He is probably the finest tactical general we have had since Wellington. But on some of his strategy, and especially on his relations with the Americans, he is almost a disaster.'

Right: General Dwight D. Eisenhower and Montgomery talk during a visit to the latter's headquarters in North Africa, 31 March 1943. Relations between these two officers were initially cordial, but eventually plumbed the depths following differences of opinion on command strategy in Northwest Europe.

WHEN WAR IS DONE

The 57-year-old Field Marshal Bernard Law Montgomery had made an undoubtedly massive contribution to Allied victory by the time the war in Europe ended in May 1945. Following the cessation of hostilities, Montgomery was at the height of his personal fame, a national figure of great importance, revered by his men and hailed as Britain's greatest soldier since Wellington. Honours were showered upon Montgomery in the UK from all quarters around the globe, including medals, swords and honorary degrees. On 1 January 1946 he was made a peer, choosing the title of Viscount Montgomery of Alamein.

The elation surrounding the end of World War II in Europe quickly ended, leaving Montgomery facing a range of difficult tasks in policing and administering occupied Germany, for which he was singularly unfit on account of his lack of training, experience and political skills. An exhausted and increasingly lonely man after the wartime members of his tactical headquarters dispersed to their homes, Montgomery's heart was not in the job. A plane crash, moreover, injured his back and Montgomery's health did not prove as robust as it had been during the war.

Montgomery returned to the UK in April 1946 and was appointed as CIGS, the highest post available in the British Army, with a two-year tenure of command. As CIGS, however, Montgomery was not a huge success in confronting a series of post-war crises and overseeing the savage post-war retrenchment of the British Army. A lack of diplomatic skills again proved a major failing in a job requiring him to work closely with politicians and the heads of the Royal Navy and Royal Air Force. Indeed, he proved a dictatorial and generally ineffective CIGS, whose small-mindedness was such he could not bring himself to sit in the same room as Air Chief Marshal Tedder, now Chief of the Air Staff (CAS), whom he could not pardon for intriguing against him at SHAEF in 1944–45. Unfortunately, in a post requiring political acumen and diplomatic skill, Monty demonstrated the same failings as he had before in Northwest Europe and many who dealt with him found him arrogant and insufferable. For fear of being outshone he deliberately tried to stop the outstanding General Sir William Slim becoming his successor. A combination of his brittle insecurity, egotism and tinge of jealousy was also reflected in his shocking and rather shabby dealings with his family and, surprisingly, with his old friends and supporters, including Francis de Guingand.

Montgomery resigned after two years as CIGS and served for the next ten years in France at the head of the Western Union Land Forces as chairman of the commanders-in-chief committee, the successor to SHAEF, with responsibility for developing a credible defence organization in the event of war with the USSR. It was a difficult appointment given that Montgomery was unable to commit the UK to Continental defence policy, and his

Field Marshal Montgomery, Marshal Rokossovsky and assembled staff at the headquarters of the 6th Airborne Division, following the link-up between British and Soviet forces on 28 April 1945.

lack of political skill did not stand him in good stead. The still-peppery Monty, however, proved to be a formidable inspector-general and oversaw a series of large-scale exercises. Unfortunately, Montgomery bickered relentlessly with his French subordinate Général Jean de Lattre de Tassigny throughout his period in office. Following the formation of the North Atlantic Treaty Organization (NATO) in 1951, Montgomery became Eisenhower's number two as Deputy Supreme Allied Commander Europe (Deputy SACEUR). Relations between Monty and Eisenhower, however, remained poor at best despite the latter's willingness to mend fences, especially without Brooke or de Guingand to mediate between the two.

Montgomery finally retired from the British Army in 1958 at the age of 71 after a career spanning 50 years. He took up residence at his home – a converted mill – at Alton in Hampshire where he lived happily for the remaining 18 years of his life. A series of world tours on peace missions immediately followed, along with speeches in the House of Lords on diverse topics including homosexuality and the support of apartheid in South Africa, as well as finishing off his highly controversial memoirs. As his health worsened Monty spent more and more time in lonely isolation at his rural home at Islington Mill. Monty's final years were bed-ridden. On 24 March 1976 he died at the age of 88. Montgomery received a state funeral at St George's Chapel at Windsor, following which he was laid to rest under a simple marble gravestone at Binstead churchyard, near his home at Alton in Hampshire.

Field Marshal Montgomery of Alamein at the War Office while CIGS, 27 October 1947. Unfortunately Montgomery did not prove to be a great success in the post, which required considerable diplomatic skill.

A LIFE IN WORDS

The controversial life and career of Field Marshal Bernard Montgomery has been discussed in hundreds of books and articles, expressing views veering between outright support and vehement criticism, and there is little sign of interest abating.

The immediate post-war view of Montgomery's generalship was very positive. A note of open criticism, however, crept in following publication of several memoirs in the US and UK discussing Allied strategy in 1944–45. A so-called 'battle of the memoirs' gathered pace following the publication of Eisenhower's *Crusade in Europe* in 1948, Omar Bradley's *A Soldier's Story* in 1951 and Bedell Smith's *Eisenhower's Six Great Decisions: Europe, 1944–1945* in 1956, which were mildly critical of Montgomery, but as a still-serving officer Montgomery did not reply in print. Montgomery's own best-selling memoirs – originally entitled *The Sparks Fly Upwards* – were published in November 1958 following his retirement. Written in a clear, lively and entertaining manner, Montgomery was characteristically boastful and showed an almost complete

Montgomery meets his two army commanders – General Omar N. Bradley and Lieutenant-General Miles Dempsey – for the first time on French soil in Normandy, 10 June 1944. Montgomery enjoyed good relations with his US Allies until criticism began to mount that he was being too slow and cautious in Normandy.

lack of magnanimity. Monty stuck unswervingly to what he perceived as being 'true', giving little or no thought to what was politic or the sensibilities of others. Montgomery presented himself throughout the book as having never made a mistake and effectively rewrote history as he believed it should be rather than as it was in order to show that everything had always gone to plan, even when this was demonstrably not the case. Little credit was given to others for their contribution to victory. Monty singled out Auchinleck and Eisenhower for scathing criticism, clearly not having forgotten or forgiven the many clashes of the past. Auchinleck was livid about Monty's frequently untrue observations and an embarrassing libel case was narrowly averted.

The US reaction to Montgomery's memoirs was predictable, with surviving participants and historians alike incensed by his claims. A furious Eisenhower – a serving US President – was profoundly wounded. It marked the end of their relationship and both soldiers barely spoke to each other again.

Monty's arrogant, overbearing and egotistical personality together with the more outrageous claims made in his memoirs made him an easy target for critics in the US and UK in the 1960s and 1970s, many claiming that he was an overrated general, with many unable or unwilling to separate his personal failings from his professional virtues. The charge in the UK against Montgomery was initially led by Correlli Barnett in his *Desert Generals*, which was highly critical of Monty in North Africa. Other books followed a similar vein, portraying Auchinleck as the victor of the first battle of El Alamein and claiming that Monty's later success was built upon the foundations laid by his predecessor.

Montgomery reacted during his last years with remarkable equanimity to the wave of hostile 'revisionist' historians, taking comfort from supporters such as Ronald Lewin. By 1976 when Montgomery died, however, his reputation had plunged to new depths. As Sir Michael Howard wrote in an obiturary, it was 'doubtful whether he will be regarded by posterity as one of the great captains of history, or even as one of the truly outstanding figures of the Second World War'.

The 1980s saw a more balanced consensus about Montgomery slowly emerge, which did not place as much emphasis on his personality, although US writers still reserved particular venom for Montgomery as a coalition general. The most notable addition to the literature was Nigel Hamilton's eulogistic authorized three-volume biography. The volumes are titled *Monty: The Making of a General, 1887–1942* (1981), *Monty: Master of the Battlefield, 1942–1944* (1984) and *Monty: The Field Marshal, 1944–1976* (1986).

The necessity for a new, balanced assessment of Montgomery's command that bridged the divide between UK and US historians was voiced during the early 1990s. Indeed, there are signs that the pendulum has at last swung back, with a largely more sympathetic view emerging on both sides of the Atlantic in accounts of his campaigns and in biographies. Stephen Hart's meticulously researched *Colossal Cracks* provides the best systematic and balanced analysis of Monty's generalship in Northwest Europe, and concludes that he was a competent general who conducted the campaign in Northwest Europe effectively given that the British Army at his disposal was a badly flawed tool. American historians have followed suit. Williamson and Murray, for example, writing in 2000, characterized him as 'one of the great field commanders of World War II', whose knowledge of training and leadership was unsurpassed. Similarly Carlo d'Este has recently characterized him as arguably World War II's most misunderstood general and has tried to put his leadership style and command into the correct perspective, especially given the flawed forces at his disposal which dictated he fought static battles employing superior firepower, *matériel* and numbers against his tactically superior opponents.

A group of assembled British and US journalists are briefed by Montgomery in Normandy in June 1944. Montgomery had an acute awareness of the power of the press and deliberately courted their attention.

Assessment

Montgomery was not a 'Great Captain', as he fervently believed himself to be, but was without doubt the best and most successful general fielded by the UK against Axis forces in Europe based on his successful wartime performance in North Africa and Northwest Europe. On balance, Montgomery was a well-rounded professional soldier on many levels by dint of experience and years of study: an impressive inspirational leader, a skilled planner who had a gift for simplifying complex problems, a great trainer of men and a talented practitioner of modern warfare, who had dedicated his life to his profession. It is difficult to disagree with historians' recent assessment that his generalship proved both competent and appropriate as GOC of Eighth Army and later 21st Army Group.

Montgomery was fortunate to reach high command in August 1942, from which point onwards the British Army enjoyed quantitative superiority in arms and equipment and was capable of considerable flexibility. It made possible the highly effective operational methods Monty had developed and which were employed at El Alamein and in Normandy, based on wearing down German fighting power by attacking on alternating axes, while at the same time remaining balanced himself with reserves and supplies held in hand for making a final decisive thrust. A sense of the practicable was one of Montgomery's greatest attributes, especially given the strengths and marked weaknesses of the forces at his disposal, and he was fully aware of the need to win the war at an acceptable cost. Montgomery realized that the wartime British Army could not fight and win on German terms and instead developed cautious operational techniques – based on carefully planned and rehearsed set-piece battles that employed surprise whenever possible, concentration,

Field Marshal Montgomery signs the unconditional surrender of the northern German armies at Luneberg Heath, 4 May 1945. It was the crowning point of Montgomery's wartime career.

overwhelming firepower and close air support – that pitted *matériel* against German tactical superiority on the battlefield. Unlike previous commanders, he imposed this approach on his subordinates, whom he had mostly picked out for their ability to command, and made sure that they had the equipment available to carry it out. This distinctive strategy – condemned as sticky and overcautious – was appropriate and fully justified, given the British Army was a wasting asset and the maintenance of morale and casualty conservation was paramount to maintain an effective army and further British war aims by being in at the kill in 1945. Montgomery implemented fast-moving armoured operations only when German opposition was dramatically reduced. Montgomery made mistakes and displayed clear failings, however, in his failure to ruthlessly exploit success, his inability to master fluid battles and his limited ability to adjust his methods to rapidly changing operational situations.

Montgomery's greatest weakness, stemming from his difficult personality, was as a coalition general, as he rose to high command at a time when the balance of power within the sometimes-fragile wartime alliance was relentlessly swinging from the UK to the US. Montgomery displayed tunnel vision by focusing far too narrowly on the purely operational military aspects of the campaign in Northwest Europe and on his self-perceived superior ability to lead rather than on the wider political-military dimension of inter-Allied cooperation. A combination of his arrogance, lack of tact, inability to compromise and the supercilious manner he displayed towards his US allies undermined cooperation and bedevilled Anglo-US relations during the closing stages of the war. It was a major failing that nearly cost him his job and which reduces his standing against other truly great British generals such as Wellington.